Public Service Employment:
A Field Evaluation

Richard P. Nathan, Robert F. Cook, V. Lane Rawlins
AND ASSOCIATES

Public Service Employment: A Field Evaluation

THE BROOKINGS INSTITUTION
Washington, D.C.

811428

Library of Congress Cataloging in Publication data:
Nathan, Richard P.
    Public service employment.
    Includes bibliographical references.
    1. Public service employment—United States.
I. Cook, Robert F., 1943–   . II. Rawlins, V. Lane.
III. Brookings Institution.   IV. Title.
HD5713.6.U54N37   331.13′77′0973   81-4596
ISBN 0-8157-5987-8 (pbk.)   AACR2

9 8 7 6 5 4 3 2 1

Foreword

IN THE 1970s Congress enacted a number of flexible, broad-gauged grants-in-aid to state and local governments that were intended by their Republican sponsors to be instruments of decentralization. The largest and most notable of these grants were for general revenue sharing (1972), employment and training (1973), and community development (1974). Each of the three has been the subject of field evaluation studies by members of the Governmental Studies staff of the Brookings Institution in collaboration with field associates. This study, which presents the findings of one of these efforts, analyzes various aspects of the public service jobs component of the Comprehensive Employment and Training Act of 1973. It explores whether federal funds merely replaced state and local funds (a matter of central concern to Congress); what the public service workers did; the extent to which the program was focused on the most disadvantaged workers; and the extent to which the program provided training and opportunities for transition to regular employment.

The study was directed by Richard P. Nathan, a ten-year veteran of the Brookings staff who joined the faculty of the Woodrow Wilson School of Public and International Affairs at Princeton University in 1979. He remains a member of the Brookings associated staff and continues to direct field research on public service employment. What is reported on here are two rounds of field observations completed in 1977 under Brookings auspices. Nathan's coauthors are Robert F. Cook, formerly a Brookings research associate and now a research economist at the Princeton Urban and Regional Research Center, and V. Lane Rawlins, professor of economics at Washington State University. The last chapter, on the role of nonprofit organizations under the public service jobs program, was written by Janet Galchick, a staff member of the Princeton Urban and Regional Research Center, and Michael Wiseman, associate professor of economics at the University of California at Berkeley. The findings presented are those of the field research associates listed on pages xiii–xv. Their on-the-scene observations are the critical element in this research. A number of people made important contributions to the work presented here. At the National Commission for Employment Policy, which supported the study under contract to the Brookings Institution, Chairman Eli Ginzberg, Director Isabel Sawhill, and staff members Patrick O'Keefe and Ralph Smith commented on reports that were submitted to the commission. The study also benefited from comments by Seymour Brandwein, director of the Office of Evaluation, U.S. Department of Labor; Martha Derthick, director of the Brookings Governmental Studies program; John Hall of Arizona State University; Susan MacManus of the University of Houston; and Steven Steib of the University of Tulsa.

Richard W. Long, Jill Ehrenreich, Linda Look, Judith Aisen, and Laura Hicks worked on this project as Brookings staff members. Computer support was provided by David Stevens of Marketing Forethought, Inc., and David Padgett of the Brookings Social Science Computation Center. Dinah Smith and Thomas Somuah, also of Brookings, prepared drafts, which were edited by David Aiken of Editorial Experts, Inc. Elaine Levkoff and Michael Padulo at Princeton University prepared the final manuscript, which was edited by Tadd Fisher of Brookings.

The authors' findings and conclusions are theirs alone and do not represent the position of the National Commission for Employment or the U.S. Department of Labor, nor should they be ascribed to the trustees, officers, or other staff members of the Brookings Institution.

BRUCE K. MAC LAURY
President

March 1981
Washington, D.C.

Contents

Text Tables

Field Research Associates and Their Jurisdictions

Bernard E. Anderson and Maureen Pirog-Good
Wharton School of Finance, University of Pennsylvania
Philadelphia, Pennsylvania

Theodore H. Curry
Michigan State University
Detroit, Michigan

Joseph M. Davis and Carol Elliott
Federation for Community Planning, Cleveland, Ohio
Cleveland, Ohio

John M. DeGrove and Deborah Athos
Joint Center for Environmental and Urban Problems, Fort Lauderdale,
    Florida
Seminole County, Florida

William O. Farber
University of South Dakota
Rapid City, South Dakota

Robert W. Gage
University of Colorado at Denver
Arapahoe County, Colorado

John S. Hall (assisted by Eleanor French Sheeler)
Arizona State University
Phoenix, Arizona; Maricopa County, Arizona

Leonard J. Hausman and Jonathan Katz
Brandeis University
Boston, Massachusetts

xiv

James F. Horan and Kenneth Palmer
University of Maine
Bangor, Maine

John S. Jackson III
Southern Illinois University
Alexander, Johnson, Massac, Pulaski, and Union counties, Illinois

James E. Jernberg
University of Minnesota
St. Paul, Minnesota

Sarah F. Liebschutz and Edward H. Downey
State University of New York
Rochester, New York

Richard W. Long
Brookings Institution
Baltimore, Maryland

William H. Lucy
University of Virginia
Charlottesville, Virginia

Susan A. MacManus
University of Houston
Houston, Texas

Rodney H. Mabry and Thomas N. Schaap
Clemson University
Anderson and Pickens counties, South Carolina

D. Beadle Moore
University of Arkansas
Conway and White counties, Arkansas

Charles J. Orlebeke
University of Illinois at Chicago Circle
Chicago, Illinois

Kay Gannon Page
Morristown, New Jersey
Morristown and Parsippany–Troy Hills Township, New Jersey

V. Lane Rawlins
Washington State University
Lane and Douglas counties, Oregon

Steve B. Steib
University of Tulsa
Tulsa, Oklahoma

Kathy Van Ness (assisted by Sandra Emerson)
University of California at Los Angeles
Los Angeles and Redondo Beach, California

F. Eugene Wagner
University of Missouri at Kansas City
Kansas City and Independence, Missouri

William D. Wagoner
University of New Orleans
New Orleans and Jefferson Parish, Louisiana

George D. Wendel and E. Allan Tomey
St. Louis University
St. Louis, University City, and Kirkwood School District, Missouri

Michael Wiseman (assisted by Sandra Threlfall)
University of California at Berkeley
San Francisco, California

CHAPTER ONE

The Public Service
Employment Program

THE PUBLIC SERVICE EMPLOYMENT (PSE) program of the federal
government, enacted by Congress in 1973 and since revised several times,
has three main goals. Like the Works Progress Administration of the depression era, it is supposed to provide jobs in a time of high unemployment. It is also intended to give employment experience to, and thereby
increase the long-run job prospects of, the "structurally unemployed,"
persons who have trouble finding jobs even in the best of times because
they lack skill and education. And it is intended to help local governments
provide needed services.

The need to balance these three major objectives—countercyclical,
structural, and public service—has caused controversy in Washington as
well as friction between the federal agency that distributes the money
(the Department of Labor) and the local and state governments that use
it. State and local officials are most interested in providing needed services, both through government agencies and private nonprofit agencies,
whereas federal officials generally focus mainly on the goal of reducing
unemployment, especially among those with low levels of education and
skill. The balance that is eventually reached reflects, in effect, a bargain
among the different levels of government: local and state officials are
willing to spend the extra time and effort needed to supervise and train
hard-to-employ persons if they see some benefits to their jurisdictions in
the form of maintaining or expanding needed services.

Because Congress did not specify what priority should be given to
each of the objectives of the public service employment program, this
bargaining process gives the program its shape. The program is constantly
changing as changes in economic and political conditions lead officials to
shift the emphasis of it. Not only is the program different from year to
year; it is also different from place to place, for it is highly decentralized

1

in form. More than 450 state and local government units receive PSE money and parcel it out to government and nonprofit agencies that employ PSE workers. No one knows the exact number of these employing agencies; in the forty jurisdictions studied under our project alone, the number of employing organizations ran into the thousands.

History and Characteristics of the Program

Publicly funded efforts to increase employment, initiated during the depression and ended when World War II made them unnecessary, were revived in the sixties as part of the antipoverty efforts of the Kennedy and Johnson administrations. During this period the main emphasis was on providing training and work experience for the economically disadvantaged. This was the goal of the Economic Opportunity Act of 1964. The Manpower Development and Training Act of 1962 likewise authorized skill training for unemployed workers, although amendments later shifted the emphasis to reducing poverty. Some programs in this field were aimed at particular geographic areas such as Appalachia, while others provided work experience for particular segments of the poverty population such as heads of families receiving welfare, older workers in rural areas, and young persons.

Following a rise in unemployment in 1969–70, the Emergency Employment Act of 1971 authorized a two-year Public Employment Program that provided funds to local governments to hire temporary workers. The groups singled out for emphasis under PEP were members of families with incomes below the poverty level, Vietnam veterans, and younger and older workers. PEP provided $1 billion in 1972 and $1.25 billion in 1973; this money paid wages for an average of 128,000 persons in those two years.

Congress passed the Comprehensive Employment and Training Act— the foundation of the contemporary public service employment program —in December 1973, and the act took effect in July 1974. CETA was designed primarily to consolidate programs aimed at various areas and population groups into a single block grant. This approach was consistent with the Nixon administration's goal of simplifying grant-in-aid programs and giving more discretion to state and local governments, which were to decide for themselves how to spend employment and training money. PEP was to be phased out and replaced by title II of CETA, which provided for a public service employment program to combat structural unemployment. A state or local jurisdiction or part of a jurisdiction was eligible for a title II grant if it was classified as experiencing "substantial unemployment"—a rate of 6.5 percent or more for three consecutive months. People were eligible to participate if they were unemployed or underemployed—that is, working only part time for economic reasons or working full time but earning less than a poverty-level income. The funds were to be paid to organizations that the act refers to as "prime sponsors."[1]

In December 1974, just half a year after CETA went into effect, Congress responded to the deepening recession by adding a new section to the act. The Emergency Jobs and Unemployment Assistance Act of 1974 established title VI of CETA as a temporary countercyclical program of public service employment. To be eligible under title VI a person had to have been unemployed for thirty days (or fifteen days if the local unemployment rate was more than 7 percent). By June 1975 title VI of CETA was providing jobs for 155,000 persons; the total of titles II and VI, plus the remainder of the PEP program that was still not phased out, brought the overall enrollment to 310,000 persons.

In 1976 Congress again made major changes when it passed the Emergency Jobs Program Extension Act. This act extended title VI and in effect created two types of title VI positions. One, known as "sustainment" positions, was designed to allow governments that had been allocated a certain number of PSE positions under the 1974 act to keep these positions. The second type was "project" positions. All new PSE workers hired under title VI had to be assigned to special projects that would last one year or less and that would not have been undertaken with local funds alone. Moreover, all new participants assigned to project positions and half the new participants assigned to fill vacancies in sustainment positions had to meet new eligibility requirements that limited title VI funds to persons who had been unemployed for fifteen of the prior twenty

1. "Prime sponsors" usually have been states or general-purpose local governments serving an area with a population of more than 100,000. Many prime sponsors, however, are consortiums of several cities or counties or both. Consortiums are especially common in suburban areas. In many states, rural areas are served by prime sponsors that cover all jurisdictions that do not run their own CETA programs or belong to a consortium; in such cases the prime sponsor is referred to as the "balance of state" prime sponsor. Each prime sponsor designates a particular operating department of the government or governments involved to administer the PSE program. They in turn allocate public service positions to other departments within participating governments, other governments such as school districts, or nonprofit organizations that serve the public.

weeks, who had exhausted their unemployment compensation payments or were receiving aid to families with dependent children (AFDC), and who had low incomes (defined as up to 70 percent of the lower-living-standard budget set by the Bureau of Labor Statistics).

The changes in 1976 were designed to reduce the amount of job displacement and fiscal substitution—that is, the use of PSE funds by local governments to replace local positions and funds. The net effect, ironically, was to give title VI—which in October 1976 supported 260,000 positions compared with only 50,000 for title II—the eligibility requirements of a structurally oriented program and to leave title II with looser criteria. In 1977, when the observations reported in this volume were made, the PSE program was operating under the regulations issued after the 1976 reauthorization of title VI.

Congress modified the program again in the fall of 1978 when it reauthorized the CETA legislation. Fiscal conservatism was rising at the time, and the PSE program was a natural target of economizers for several reasons. It was one of the biggest and fastest growing of all federal grant-in-aid programs. Local news media were uncovering instances of mismanagement, such as ineligible participants or cases of nepotism. And critics continued to suspect that PSE funds were simply replacing local spending.

Under the law enacted that year the PSE program that had been known as title II was renumbered title II-D and aimed more narrowly at persons suffering long-term unemployment for structural reasons. It was also modified to put more emphasis on training and placement to help participants find permanent jobs in the private job market. A person could participate in this program who had been unemployed for at least fifteen of the previous twenty weeks or who was receiving AFDC *and* was economically disadvantaged (which means generally that the person came from a family earning less than 70 percent of the lower living standard).

Title VI retained the distinction between project and sustainment jobs. Half of the title VI participants had to be assigned to projects scheduled to last eighteen months or less; the other half had to be assigned to entry-level jobs in regular government departments or nonprofit agencies. Persons would be eligible for title VI jobs if they had been unemployed for at least ten of the previous twelve weeks *and* if their families had incomes no larger than the lower-standard-of-living budget or received AFDC.

The 1978 reauthorization also set limits on the wages that could be paid to PSE participants for any position ($10,000 maximum, $7,200 for the average of all positions) and on the length of time a person could remain in the PSE program (eighteen months, although the Department of Labor could grant waivers to individual sponsors for all or part of their participants).

In March 1978 enrollment in titles II and VI reached a peak as a result of being bolstered by President Carter's 1977 economic stimulus package, which added $4 billion to the fiscal year 1978 budget for PSE. Over 750,000 persons were employed, equal to 10 percent of all unemployed persons in the labor force. Outlays reached $5.6 billion in fiscal year 1978. Since then the size of the program has been reduced. The average PSE enrollment in fiscal 1978 was 680,000; the average for fiscal 1979 was 557,000. At the end of fiscal year 1980, 328,000 persons were enrolled.

Approach of This Study

This study concentrates on the PSE program's intergovernmental effects rather than its effects on individual jobholders. It addresses such questions as whether the program creates jobs in local governments, whether local governments give preference to the disadvantaged, and what kinds of services are provided. Succeeding chapters deal with public service employment as countercyclical policy (chapter 2), as structural policy (chapter 3), and as a vehicle for providing needed public services at the state and local level (chapter 4). The final chapter considers nonprofit organizations as employers of PSE participants.

The study was conducted in a representative sample of jurisdictions by a network of field researchers in cooperation with a small central staff based in Washington at the Brookings Institution. The central staff chose the field staff members (designated "associates") for their knowledge of local public finances and institutions and of the particular areas of government activity under study. None of the associates were officially connected with the jurisdictions in the sample. All were residents of the area they studied and devoted an average of thirty to sixty days to their participation in the field study. Half of the associates were political scientists and half were economists. Their names and jurisdictions are listed on pages xiii–xv.

Associates worked with the central staff in developing a common analytical framework and research design. Using this design, the associates then reported their observations of the effects of PSE in their jurisdictions.

Members of the central staff maintained contact with the associates, reviewed and coded the field data, and analyzed and compiled the overall results.[2] This study is based on findings from observations in July 1977, when PSE was being expanded by the added funds from President Carter's economic stimulus package, and in December 1977, when the buildup was nearly complete.[3]

We used a representative rather than a random sample of governmental jurisdictions for several reasons. One reason is that there is no list of the universe of governmental jurisdictions receiving PSE funds from which a random sample might be drawn. Moreover, we wanted to include in the study a cross section of types of recipient jurisdictions—large cities (both fiscally distressed and economically healthy), suburban jurisdictions, and rural jurisdictions. Finally, to make it feasible (for efficiency's sake) for most field associates to cover more than one jurisdiction, it was necessary to choose sample jurisdictions that were close to each other—for example, a central city and its overlying county, or three or four rural towns reasonably near a university having an economic or governmental research center. Because a number of large jurisdictions were included, the sample jurisdictions as a whole accounted for approximately 10 percent of PSE enrollees.

2. Using the same general technique, a field studies group in the Governmental Studies program at Brookings has studied general revenue sharing and community development block grants as well as the PSE program. For a more detailed description of the method, see Richard P. Nathan, "The Methodology for Field Network Evaluation Studies," in Walter Williams, ed., *Studying Implementation* (Chatham, N.J.: Chatham House, forthcoming), chap. 4. For findings from the other programs, see Richard P. Nathan, Allen D. Manvel, Susannah E. Calkins, and Associates, *Monitoring Revenue Sharing* (Brookings Institution, 1975); Richard P. Nathan, Charles F. Adams, Jr., and Associates, *Revenue Sharing: The Second Round* (Brookings Institution, 1977); Paul R. Dommel and others, *Targeting Community Development* (U.S. Department of Housing and Urban Development, January 1980); Dommel and others, *Decentralizing Community Development* (U.S. Department of Housing and Urban evelopment, 1978); and Richard P. Nathan and others, *Block Grants for Community Development* (U.S. Department of Housing and Urban Development, 1977). An earlier report of PSE findings is contained in Richard P. Nathan and others, *Monitoring the Public Service Employment Program* (National Commission for Manpower Policy, March 1978).

3. Field studies of PSE have continued at the project's new base, the Urban and Regional Research Center at the Woodrow Wilson School of Public and International Affairs, Princeton University. A third round of observations was done in December 1979 and a fourth round in December 1980. See note 1 of the epilogue to this study.

CHAPTER TWO

Combating Cyclical Unemployment

ONE OF THE MOST important purposes, if not the predominant purpose, of the public service employment program under the Comprehensive Employment and Training Act of 1973 has been to create new jobs in order to put unemployed persons to work during times of recession or slow economic growth. Because CETA puts most spending decisions in the hands of local governments, there has been understandable concern that these governments might simply replace locally financed positions with federally funded ones. If localities were to do this, the result would be more like revenue sharing than a job creation program. Congressional concern over this issue has been so strong that in 1977 after a lengthy debate centering around this issue of displacement, the Senate came within thirteen votes of deleting an increase of 415,000 public service jobs from the Carter administration's $13.5 billion economic stimulus package.

The concern about displacement arises from the nature of the problem —a recession—and the nature of the solution—a decentralized program. During a recession state and local governments face declines in tax receipts. Government officials need to look for ways to save money in a relatively short time, preferably in ways that do not require legislative action. This often involves the personnel budget, which in most jurisdictions makes up a major part of the government's expenses. Many local governments put a hold on new hiring or cut back the number of employees through layoffs or attrition. At the same time, the federal government is providing new or additional funding that is supposed to create jobs to counter the recession. Local governments have a great deal of leeway on how to spend that money. The logical result is a potential conflict between the federal government's goal of job creation and the local government's need to relieve fiscal strain.

Two primary questions arise. First, to what extent have local and state governments actually created new positions and hired unemployed persons who would not have been hired without federal funds, as opposed to using federal money to fill jobs that would have existed anyway? This is the primary question we will deal with. The second question, related to the first, is how jurisdictions have used the local money that has been freed by the receipt of federal public service employment funds. The first question deals with the employment effects of PSE, the second question with its related fiscal effects. This chapter covers the first at some length and the second more briefly.

Before we discuss these two questions, a third one should be mentioned. Does the PSE program cause governments to hire workers, such as women, minorities, and people with limited education, whom they would not have hired in the absence of federal funds? That is, will PSE have a long-run effect on the composition of the work force? We tried to gather information on this topic in our two rounds of research. Disentangling the effect of PSE from the effects of other factors is difficult at best, but some generalizations are possible.

We know that in the short term cities are quick to include the many women and minorities among PSE workers in the statistics on municipal employees that they send to the Equal Employment Opportunity Commission, as evidence that they are improving the opportunities for these groups. As to the longer term, we know that many of the PSE workers who make the transition to regular jobs in the government stay in the agencies where they were first assigned. We can deduce that eventually these people will grow in numbers and will affect the composition of these agencies, but we cannot show that changes are caused by PSE because affirmative action programs are also having some effect.

We have also found some evidence that dealing with PSE employees has led some jurisdictions to discover that they can usefully employ many people eligible for subsidized positions in regular jobs—for example, that a person does not need a high school diploma to work on a sanitation truck. Here are excerpts of reports from associates in two cities that illustrate this development:

In our opinion, CETA has demonstrated to the city that hiring disadvantaged workers can be done successfully if attention is paid to problems of management. Perhaps the most important service provided by CETA has been the "sensitivity" training program which has been provided for managers and foremen on the worksites in which CETA employees have been located. This training, according to observers, has "spilled over" and generally improved attitudes toward minority and hard-to-employ recruitment.

                              *   *   *

The city's policy regarding new hires for entry-level positions is that only PSE participants are hired. Every entry-level position is filled with PSE participants moving to permanent city employment. Consequently, the composition of the new hires is almost identical to the composition of the PSE labor force.

Research Approach and Definitions

The field associates gathered information on the employment and fiscal effects of PSE in forty jurisdictions and were asked to use information obtained in five ways:

1. Interviews with officials of the jurisdiction. This source was of limited usefulness because the federal government's legal ban on the use of funds for displacement inhibited local officials from talking candidly, even though they were assured under our agreement with the Department of Labor that we would not publish data on displacement for any particular jurisdiction and that the information gathered would not be used for enforcement purposes. Although many officials remained reluctant to discuss the displacement issue, others provided important information and insights on the program's net employment effects.

2. Observations of the actual tasks performed by PSE participants and interviews with first-line supervisors at job sites.

3. Examination of overall budget and employment conditions and trends.

4. Examination of budget and employment data and trends for the agencies in which PSE participants were employed.

5. Assessment of any changes in public demand for the services being provided by the government.

In some of the larger jurisdictions the large number of agencies and projects employing PSE workers made it impossible to observe the tasks of all workers or to interview all supervisors. Instead, we used a sampling technique that is described in the appendix.

Describing an approach that was fairly typical of that of the other associates, an associate in a large city told how he gathered information:

The importance of each type of data has varied depending on the type of employing agencies, availability of data, and our own experience.

With PSE positions in city departments we placed a heavy emphasis on the overall fiscal conditions along with information on budget and employment patterns and assessments by local officials, the latter two types given equal but secondary weight. Finally, we took the overall fiscal condition into account.

For the smaller not-for-profit agencies and neighborhood organizations, our evaluations relied heavily on the specific tasks performed by PSE participants and the demand for services. Discussions with agency personnel helped clarify data questions and aided in identifying problems in subcontracting procedure. Finally, patterns of employment were also considered.

Before the research began, field associates and central staff for the research project agreed on the following definitions of what constitutes job creation and displacement:

JOB CREATION

New programs and services. Cases in which additional programs or services were provided with PSE funding that would not otherwise have been undertaken.

Special projects. New, one-time projects lasting one year or less that were undertaken with PSE funds.

Program expansion. Cases in which the level of service was raised or services were improved under existing programs by using PSE funding.

Program maintenance. Cases in which PSE employees were used to maintain services that would have been curtailed without PSE funding.

JOB DISPLACEMENT

Transfers. Cases involving the transfer of existing state and local government positions to PSE funding.

Rehires. Cases in which the government laid off regular employees and then rehired them with PSE funding.

Contract reduction. Cases in which PSE participants were used to provide services or to work on projects that had been, or normally would be, contracted to an outside organization or private firm.

Potential hires. Cases in which PSE participants were hired to fill positions that otherwise would have been funded with other revenue.

Our definition of "special projects" is more restrictive than the definition in the law. Under the law, as of 1977 all title VI public service employment above the sustainment level had to be devoted to projects with a duration of one year or less. Local officials could use these projects, however, to expand or maintain programs where they could demonstrate that the programs would otherwise have been cut or kept at a constant level. In this study we limit the definition of special projects as a subcategory of job creation to *new* activities; this definition does not include projects that expand or avoid reduction in ongoing programs.

PSE Program Changes during the Observation Period

The period between the first observation in July 1977 and the second observation in December of that year was a time of growth and change for the PSE program nationally as the Carter economic stimulus package was implemented. The analysis takes into account the following developments in these six months:

—The number of positions filled with PSE funds more than doubled, from 310,000 to 626,000 nationally. (The jurisdictions covered in our research employed a total of 61,828 PSE workers in December, or about 10 percent of the national total.)

—Project positions increased their share of the total in the sample, from about one-fourth in July to about half in December. The term "project" is used here in the way it is used in the law—anything that provides an employment level or enrollment beyond what existed in titles II and VI before the expansion of the program.

—The principal governments—that is, governments that directly received PSE money—retained a smaller share of all PSE workers for their own departments. In July they were keeping 70 percent of all positions; in December they were retaining only 52 percent. This increased practice of subcontracting PSE workers to other agencies affected both sustainment and project positions. The percentage of sustainment positions retained by the principal governments in the sample dropped from 79 percent to 65 percent; the percentage of project positions, from 59 percent to 35 percent.

—Many of the positions the principal governments did not retain went to nonprofit organizations, which in the jurisdictions studied increased their overall share of PSE positions from 13 percent in July to 25 percent in December. Workers assigned to nonprofit organizations accounted for more than two-fifths (43 percent) of the project positions in December. School districts also increased their share of PSE workers, from 7 percent in July (when the schools were not in session) to 13 percent in December. The proportion of positions assigned to other employing agencies remained essentially constant between the two observations. Table 2-1 shows where the PSE workers in the sample jurisdictions were assigned in December.

Factors other than the changes in composition of the program noted above were affecting PSE during this period. At the time of the December observation many officials of local and state governments were uncertain about the future of the PSE program because during the fall of 1977 members of the Carter administration were talking about converting PSE into a program of minimum-wage jobs tied to welfare reform. Moreover, CETA was up for reauthorization in the spring of 1978, and some members of Congress were advocating making drastic changes in

Table 2-1. *Distribution of Public Service Employment Participants in the Sample Jurisdictions, December 1977*

Percent

Agency	Sustainment positions	Project positions	Total
Principal governments	65	35	52
School districts	14	12	13
Other local governments	6	6	6
State agencies	4	3	4
Federal agencies	*	1	*
Nonprofit organizations	10	43	25
Total	100	100	100
Addenda:			
Number of positions	33,785	28,043	61,828
Percentage of total	54	46	100

Source: Data reported by Brookings field associates. Figures are rounded.
* Less than 0.5 percent.

the program or reducing or even eliminating it because of concern over the issues of displacement and ineligible participants. In this situation many local governments were hesitant to rely on PSE to supply workers for basic services and consequently were more likely to subcontract workers to other agencies.

Employment Effects

As a result of the changes in the composition of the PSE program and the uncertainty about its future, the proportion of all jobs due to job creation increased and the proportion due to displacement accordingly decreased between July and December 1977.

Following are the percentages of all PSE jobs (both those retained by principal governments and those farmed out) that the field associates found represented displacement in the sample jurisdictions for each observation:

	Sustainment positions	Project positions	Overall
July	21	8	18
December	19	10	15

Table 2-2. *Distribution of Public Service Net Employment Effects by Type of Position, December 1977*
Percent

Effect	Sustainment positions	Project positions	Overall
Job creation	**81**	**90**	**85**
New services	9	19	14
Expansion of existing services	47	40	44
Special projects	3	24	13
Program maintenance	22	6	15
Job displacement	**19**	**10**	**15**
Transfers	5	*	3
Rehires	*	*	*
Potential hires	12	8	10
Contract reduction	1	1	. . .
Other	1	*	*
Total	100	100	100

Source: Data reported by Brookings field associates. Figures are rounded.
* Less than 0.5 percent.

Even though the rate of displacement increased slightly among project positions, this rate remained lower than that for sustainment positions. Because a much larger share of all positions went to project positions than to sustainment positions, the overall displacement rate dropped slightly between July and December.

As of December 1977, then, when the PSE program was well into a period of tremendous growth resulting from the Carter administration's economic stimulus package, 85 percent of PSE jobs in our sample jurisdictions represented job creation and 15 percent were classified as displacement. The rate of displacement was about twice as high for sustainment positions—one in five—as for project positions—one in ten.[1]

Table 2-2 indicates what contributed to these overall rates. It shows what proportions of PSE jobs fit into each of the four categories of job creation and four categories of displacement in the judgment of the field associates.

1. Although most sustainment positions had been in place for the longest period of time (most of the title VI sustainment positions had been filled since at least October 1976), title II doubled in size during the buildup and so some part of the title II and title VI sustainment positions included here are relatively recent additions.

Job Creation

The most common type of job creation was the expansion of services, such as longer hours for a government office. More than two PSE positions out of every five (44 percent) were used for this purpose in the sample jurisdictions at the time of the December observation. This fact is not surprising; at a time when the PSE program was adding many new participants, governments found it easier to add workers to agencies and increase the level of services those agencies provided than to undertake new activities or to plan new projects and services.

This report from a field associate in a rural town describes the approach of many jurisdictions, both large and small:

No wholly new services were provided with PSE positions, and no positions were used to maintain services which otherwise would have been reduced. The town adopted a middle-ground job creation strategy: create jobs that involve the performance of important tasks with identifiable termination points. Do not establish new services, services which require additional supervisors, or services which may acquire their own constituency of supporters. Also, do not use PSE to maintain services, because in the absence of PSE, resistance to reducing the service level would be substantial.

Governments used a smaller proportion of PSE workers to continue an existing level of service ("program maintenance") in December than they had in July. This drop is a result of the rise in the proportion of project positions, whch governments seldom used simply to maintain current service levels. It also reflects the increase in the proportion of sustainment positions that governments subcontract to outside employers.

The use of PSE workers to expand existing services leads all other uses for both sustainment and project workers. The figures for the other uses generally conform to congressional intentions for each type of position. Governments used a significant share of sustainment positions to maintain programs at their current levels, and used sizable proportions of project positions to provide new services or to help with what field researchers defined as special one-time projects that were due to end in a year or less. As noted earlier, our definition of special projects differs from that of the Department of Labor; only one-fourth of what the government calls project positions actually are assigned to what we call special projects.

The following is from an associate in a distressed large city:

The number of jobs created per dollar invested seems to differ dramatically between sustainment and project PSE. The job creation effect is particularly high in CBO [community-based organizations] projects. The fact that government projects have a higher rate of job creation than government sustainment PSE, but a lower creation rate than CBOs, is not at all surprising. Certain city departments, particularly the ones with relatively small numbers of PSE participants, distinguish carefully between project and sustainment workers. The two types of workers often perform strikingly different tasks. These projects, such as a new computerization project or outreach of social service agencies to a new neighborhood, represent the bulk of job creation in the city government. However, only a small percentage of PSE project workers are involved in projects of this nature in city government, the vast majority (in our sample) are in projects nearly identical to the work of sustainment hires. This is corroborated by the fact that there are so many intertitle transfers. The workers are viewed as homogeneous labor. On the other hand, most CBO projects (in our sample) either represent a true expansion of services to a broader clientele or consist of workers who are deemed so marginal that the sponsoring organizations would need to curtail their activities only very slightly in the absence of these workers.

Our finding that governments often use project PSE positions to expand existing services rather than assign them to special projects may explain the increase in displacement for project PSE employees. The following excerpt from a report by an associate in a large city illustrates this pattern:

The result of the PSE program in the city thus far has been job creation. The types of PSE jobs created within city government have largely been laborer, clerical, or service jobs. Most of the job creation within city government has been in the primary service areas—public works (sewage, garbage), street repair, and parks and recreation—and has represented expansion of services rather than creation of new services or special projects. (This applies to both title II and title VI—sustainment and special projects.) This is the case because the city has traditionally been understaffed and its normal rate of employee growth has basically allowed the city to "stay even" with service demands— to maintain existing service levels, but not to "get ahead." Thus, many of the PSE participants are put to work doing things that, while they might not seem like expansion of services to the outside observer, represent expansion. They are services that have often been planned but have never been implemented due to lack of funds and personnel. This is largely attributable to the local political environment which dictates that the city maintain a large budget surplus and a stable tax rate at the expense, if necessary, of increased service and personnel levels.

Job creation within the CBOs has increasingly represented expansion of services rather than special projects or new services. The reason for this is that the pressure from the PSE coordinator to meet hiring quotas has been best achieved by contacting and then contracting with larger, *established* nonprofit social service-type agencies (who are traditionally short on funds but more than willing to expand services if funds or personnel become available).

Displacement

The most common kind of displacement is the category of potential hires, both in the sustainment and the project parts of the program. The associate for a large city reported what obtains in many jurisdictions:

The effect of displacement is to hold down the number of personnel which the city would otherwise hire to expand or maintain services. There are no dramatic effects that I have been able to discern. Mostly, agencies seem to begin by buying a little temporary budget flexibility. Some appear to cross the line into displacement quite inadvertently.

From another large city:

In most cases, displacement in this sample seems to be a result of hiring individuals for jobs which would have been created without PSE. Several subcontractors of all major types, for example, have used PSE participants to staff new facilities or programs which would have required regularly budgeted employees in the absence of this funding source. In other cases, hiring of clerical and other workers for projects which are not fully underway and/or assigning them less than full time to PSE activities and projects has produced some displacement. This latter type of displacement seems particularly easy with clerical, maintenance and similar positions with easily transferable skills.

While all of these instances seem likely to be consciously planned displacement, more obvious forms such as hiring of former employees and transferring workers to the PSE payroll were not observed. But, considering the city's literal interpretation of regulations and fairly careful monitoring of eligibility, it seems unlikely that the city would have allowed any of these more easily traceable forms of displacement. In addition, given this monitoring, rehiring or transferring would require a chain of cooperative conspirators from the level of department supervisors to the PSE unit.

The rates of displacement in table 2-2 are for all PSE positions, those retained by the governments in the sample as well as those assigned by those governments to other agencies. Below are the displacement rates (in percents) calculated separately for the PSE workers the governments retained for their own departments:

	Sustainment positions	*Project positions*	*Overall*
July	24	7	21
December	23	18	22

The changes among retained positions basically parallel those among all PSE positions. Displacement rose among project positions but remained lower than the rate among sustainment positions; because project positions took a large share of all positions, the overall displacement remained essentially the same for the two observation periods.

In evaluating these changes, we kept two things in mind. First, the July and December observations occurred in the same fiscal year for many of the jurisdictions in our sample. Other researchers have suggested that displacement is likely to increase with each new budget cycle as government officials take stock of the services PSE workers are providing and decide whether or not to hire more regular workers or to keep existing ones. If this suggestion is true, and it at least makes good sense, then a later observation is likely to show a higher displacement rate, other things being equal.

The second point is that because the figures for the sustainment part of the program include positions authorized under title II as well as the sustainment portion of title VI, the rate of displacement for sustainment positions is affected by the large rise in the number of title II positions during this period. The increase in the number of new title II positions may have held down the amount of displacement observed. Again, in a stable program displacement seems likely to increase over time.

Employment Effects by Class of Jurisdiction

In this section the data are analyzed separately for each of the following four classes of jurisdictions for the PSE positions they retained for their own departments:

Distressed large cities. Central cities with more than 250,000 residents that rated relatively high on an index of urban distress, developed by members of the field study group.[2]

Other large cities. Central cities with more than 250,000 population that rated relatively low on the urban conditions index, that is, were relatively well off.

Suburban. Smaller cities (the largest being a suburban city of 112,000) and suburban counties.

2. For a discussion of the urban conditions index used to rate urban distress see Paul R. Dommel and others, *Decentralizing Community Development* (U.S. Department of Housing and Urban Development, 1978), app. 2. A distressed large city was defined as one with a rating of 250 or more on this index. The index is constructed by multiplying a standardized percentage of the population in poverty by the standardized percentage of pre-1940 housing and dividing the product by the standardized percentage of population change from 1960 to 1975.

PUBLIC SERVICE EMPLOYMENT

Table 2-3. *Distribution of Public Service Net Employment Effects by Class of Jurisdiction, Principal Governments Only, December 1977*

Percent

Effect	Distressed large cities	Other large cities	Suburban	Rural	Total
Job creation	**69**	**89**	**81**	**82**	**78**
New services	7	16	10	4	11
Expansion of existing services	24	51	45	52	38
Special project	7	12	12	17	9
Program maintenance	30	10	13	9	20
Job displacement	**31**	**11**	**19**	**18**	**22**
Total	100	100	100	100	100

Source: Data reported by Brookings field associates. Figures are rounded.
* Less than 0.5 percent.

Rural. Rural cities and towns outside metropolitan areas with populations of less than 50,000; counties outside metropolitan areas (the largest with a population of 105,000), and a state agency in a balance-of-state area.

As indicated in table 2-3, the distressed large cities had the highest overall displacement rate; as of December 1977 they used 31 percent of their PSE positions to avoid hiring more regular workers or for other purposes classed by the associates as displacement. These same cities used another 30 percent of their PSE positions to maintain program levels. This rate of program maintenance was three times higher than the rate for the other large cities in the study. In the distressed large cities 12 percent of the project positions and 39 percent of the sustainment positions were considered to be maintaining existing services.

These figures are not surprising; we expected that the financially hard-pressed large cities would most readily yield to the temptation to use PSE funds for fiscal relief. These cities typically also have high unemployment rates, however, and thus have the greatest need for job creation through a program like PSE. We included a disproportionately large number of these cities in our sample precisely because we wanted to see how they were responding to these conflicting pressures.

Here is an associate's report on a financially pressed large city:

The most important factor to recognize in analyzing the PSE job creation effort is the severe financial constraint which faces the city, its quasi-governmental agencies, and CBOs. The basic fact is that the city would have to cut back in a number of areas without the assistance of PSE funds. Other agencies, such as the Housing Authority and CBOs, are in essentially the same situation. Those organizations have limited budgets, or in the case of CBOs, virtually no funding whatsoever. It follows that programmatic needs attendant on financial hardships exerted a significant influence over the types of jobs that were created under PSE; again, here, as noted above, PSE slots were often used to maintain or provide basic services.

The high rate of displacement in distressed large cities compares with rates of 11 percent for large cities that were not financially distressed, 19 percent for suburban jurisdictions, and 18 percent for rural governments. For all classes of jurisdictions taken together, the rate of displacement among positions that the governments retain for their own use was 22 percent.

Employment Effects by Degree of Fiscal Pressure

The sample governments were also divided into groups according to the degree of fiscal pressure they faced, that is, to what extent local tax receipts were dropping while demands for services were rising. The four levels of fiscal pressure we used are "none" (shown by three jurisdictions), "relatively little" (shown by six), "moderate" (shown by thirteen), and "extreme" (shown by fourteen). Because the classification of fiscal pressure is for the sample governments, only the PSE positions within the governments are included.

In assessing the degree of fiscal pressure a jurisdiction faces, associates were asked to consider two kinds of information. First was the objective fiscal situation as shown by trends in year-end cash balances, rates of growth in taxes and expenditures, the presence or absence of fund deficits, the use of short-term borrowing, increases or decreases in the tax base, bond rating, and increases or decreases in nominal tax rates. The second kind of information was more subjective; included here are assessments by local officials of the capacity to expand activities or add new programs or services; evidence of increasing demands for services, either from the public or from mandates from other governments; signs of a local tax revolt or refusal to pass a tax or bond referendum; and constraints on the ability to increase taxes.

"Fiscal pressure," as used here, is thus not the same as "distress," as that term is used in connection with indexes of urban distress. A city could be expanding its population and tax base, and thus not be distressed, but could nonetheless face a great deal of fiscal pressure. This could hap-

Table 2-4. *Distribution of Public Service Net Employment Effects by Degree of Fiscal Pressure, Employees of Principal Governments Only, Titles II and VI*

Percent

	Degree of fiscal pressure on jurisdiction			
Effect	*None*	*Relatively little*	*Moderate*	*Extreme*
Job creation	**72**	**87**	**81**	**77**
New services	11	11	10	10
Expansion of existing services	45	41	45	31
Special projects	11	24	17	10
Program maintenance	5	12	9	25
Job displacement	**28**	**13**	**19**	**23**
Total	100	100	100	100
Addendum:				
Number of governments	3	6	13	14

Source: Data reported by Brookings field associates. Figures are rounded.

pen if new residents and businesses were demanding expanded services and new facilities while voters were refusing to approve any increases in tax rates that were necessary to pay for those services and facilities.

As table 2-4 shows, the highest average displacement rates occurred for jurisdictions with no fiscal pressure (28 percent) and those with extreme fiscal pressure (23 percent). The displacement rate among those with relatively little fiscal pressure was 13 percent and among those with moderate fiscal pressure 19 percent.

The results of the study of the general revenue sharing program show a similar U-shaped pattern for the substitution uses of revenue sharing funds.[3] Jurisdictions facing extreme fiscal pressure would be most likely to regard PSE funding as a form of fiscal relief, that is, as a means of lowering or stabilizing taxes. At the other end of the fiscal pressure spectrum, the governments in this study that faced no fiscal pressure tended to be very conservative on fiscal matters. These jurisdictions gauge their fiscal health not by the existence of a surplus but by its size. Under these conditions it is not surprising that officials would be tempted to use PSE

3. Richard P. Nathan, Charles F. Adams, Jr., and Associates, *Revenue Sharing: The Second Round* (Brookings Institution, 1977), pp. 33 ff.

funding as an alternative to raising taxes to meet an increasing level of services required by population growth.

Creating jobs for purposes of program maintenance is closely related to fiscal pressure. The rate of program maintenance was highest (25 percent) for those jurisdictions that faced extreme fiscal pressure and lowest (5 percent) for those facing no fiscal pressure, although almost half of the positions in jurisdictions with extreme fiscal pressure represented either program maintenance or displacement. In contrast, jurisdictions with no fiscal pressure tended to concentrate their PSE positions on the expansion of existing activities (45 percent). Jurisdictions facing relatively little or moderate fiscal pressure tended to use considerably more of their PSE positions for special projects than did other jurisdictions.

According to an associate in a suburban county facing no fiscal pressure:

The special project job creation activities under title VI really are different from sustainment positions in most of the public agencies. There is a clear intent to set up jobs that will be self-expiring when a particular task is completed. But, without access to capital and with limitations on supervisors, there is a difficulty in dreaming up new ideas that don't seem totally ludicrous. There are a great number of data processing, recataloging, filing, recoding kinds of projects that are related to improvement of the way information is handled. Some real limits are being reached because of the lack of office space, desks, and other equipment.

Jurisdictions facing no fiscal pressure were more likely to cause displacement by transferring regular employees to PSE funding than were other jurisdictions (14 percent of PSE workers in the jurisdictions facing little pressure, 5 percent in those facing moderate pressure, and 4 percent in those facing extreme pressure). This is because when the field associates decided that local funds would have been available to continue to support transferred jobs, they classified such use of PSE positions as displacement. In contrast, a jurisdiction facing extreme fiscal pressure might transfer positions that had been supported locally as an alternative to abolishing them; the associates classified such shifts as program maintenance, and thus job creation.

Other Types of Employing Organizations

Local governments used two kinds of arrangements for PSE participants employed outside the sample governments: subcontracting and "outstationing."

A PSE worker who is "outstationed" is paid by a government and counted as an employee of that government but in fact works for some other entity or agency. Generally this is an administrative arrangement that allows smaller organizations lacking payroll systems to employ PSE employees but have their wages paid by the government that does the outstationing. In other cases, particularly in the smaller jurisdictions, it is done as a matter of administrative convenience. In the second round of the field study 4 percent of the PSE participants in the sample jurisdictions were outstationed by the sample governments.

Far more common is the practice of subcontracting positions to other government and nongovernment organizations. Under subcontracting arrangements, PSE participants are employees of the subcontracting agency and are paid by that agency, which is reimbursed on a contractual basis by the sponsor government. Forty-four percent of the positions in the sample jurisdictions were subcontracted to other organizations in the second round—30 percent of the sustainment positions and 60 percent of the project positions.

An associate described how one large city handled placement in other agencies:

Both sorts of arrangements come up. By and large the CETA office operates with outstationing arrangements with federal and state offices and the housing and redevelopment authorities. All CBO projects are conducted on a subcontracting basis unless they are established in city agencies. Basically what subcontracting does is to transfer the responsibility for selecting employees to the subcontracted agency. For other positions—the outstationed ones—the CETA office directly intervenes in the hiring.

As pointed out earlier, a notable change from the first round to the second was the increase in subcontracting and outstationing of PSE positions. Although the size of the PSE program roughly doubled in this six-month period, a large part of this increase occurred in the number of positions assigned to organizations outside the sample governments. Between July and December some of the sample jurisdictions actually reduced the number of PSE employees in their own departments and agencies. Instead, they subcontracted or outstationed their positions to other organizations. This was particularly true for project positions.

The governments in this study subcontracted PSE positions to several types of employment organizations—other local governments, nonprofit organizations, school districts, state agencies, and federal agencies. This spreading of positions among government and, more important, nongovernment agencies that has occurred with growth is an important program effect that has not been widely noted in the literature. The sections that follow discuss each of these other types of sponsoring organizations.

OTHER LOCAL GOVERNMENTS. Many governments in the study subcontracted positions to other local governments, both general-purpose units and special districts and authorities. The governments in the study, it should be recalled, were either jurisdictions that are themselves prime sponsors or are part of a larger prime sponsor (consortium or balance of state) and receive a direct allocation of positions from the sponsor.

At the time of the second observation the jurisdictions in the study had assigned 6 percent of their total PSE allocations to other units of local government. This was the same percentage as in the first round. But the overall number of positions had more than doubled; for project positions, the number had more than tripled. The extent of subcontracting to other local governments varied by the type of sample jurisdiction. Large cities subcontracted less than 5 percent of their total positions to other units of government; often these units were park and water districts, which are closely related to the subcontracting jurisdiction. Many of the suburban and rural jurisdictions in the sample are counties and hence tend to have more units of general purpose governments within their boundaries. These jurisdictions subcontracted slightly more than 20 percent of their PSE positions to other units of government.

Of the more than 3,400 positions assigned to other units of local government, the largest proportions were assigned to cities and towns by county governments. Almost as many positions were assigned to housing authorities, although these positions were concentrated in the housing authorities of a few large cities. The activities of these workers included maintaining public housing units, clearing and boarding up vacant housing, and cleaning vacant land owned by the housing authority. These two categories, along with universities and community colleges,[4] accounted for 80 percent of the positions in other units of local government. Other types of jurisdictions included sewer and water districts, transit authorities, and park and planning districts.

Ten percent of the positions in other units of local government were classified as displacement. The increase in the number of newly created positions in these agencies apparently held down the displacement rate. In the first round of the study, the displacement rate among other units of local government was almost the same as in the sample governments.

4. Universities in this case were most often city and county institutions (colleges and junior colleges) organized on a special district basis.

NONPROFIT ORGANIZATIONS. By December the recipients of the largest number of subcontracted positions were nonprofit organizations, accounting for one-fourth of all PSE participants in the second round of the study, including 10 percent of the sustainment positions and 43 percent of the project positions. In all, almost 1,800 nonprofit organizations had PSE positions. The average number of participants in an agency was eight, but this differed by title. Among sustainment positions the average was slightly more than three per agency. By contrast, the average number of PSE participants per agency in title VI projects was found to be higher—approximately ten. In any agency the range was from one to 120.

In considering the data on nonprofit organizations it should be remembered that at the time of the first field observations project positions had been in place for no more than two months. Although some of these participants were still employed in December, most PSE positions in nonprofit organizations were recent additions and had been in place less than seven months.

For nonprofit organizations as a whole, the displacement rate for the second round was 4 percent, much less than the 22 percent rate for PSE participants employed directly by governments in this study. Project employees in nonprofit organizations were more likely than project participants employed by the governments in this study to be engaged in providing new services (20 percent and 24 percent, respectively) and expanding existing services (25 percent and 43 percent, respectively).

Relatively few employees in nonprofit organizations worked in what we define as special projects. For both sustainment and project positions in nonprofit organizations, the proportions in special projects were lower than for PSE participants employed directly by the governments in the sample. What these figures indicate, and what the associates report, is that most jobs were created within nonprofit organizations by expanding activities rather than by adding new activities. A drug counseling agency, for example, was likely to use PSE positions to expand the amount of counseling it does or to provide the service in new areas rather than to provide entirely new services.

The associate in a large city reported:

In the category of non-city PSE are neighborhood organizations, the Urban League, and the Salvation Army. As a general rule this type of agency will decrease, maintain, expand, or develop its services depending on the availability of funds. Although many of these agencies would hope to continue projects or services begun under PSE funding, virtually none would be able to do so simply because of the lack of money.

Although the associates did not collect data on the topic, they saw some indication that in some nonprofit organizations part-time unpaid volunteers were replaced by full-time PSE participants. In some cases these were the same persons. We considered such replacement to be job creation because it does provide a paid job where none existed before. By standard sponsor definition, someone who has been doing unpaid work is unemployed or underemployed and hence eligible. Whether this is consistent with the spirit of the act is another matter.

SCHOOL DISTRICTS. By December 1977, school districts were second only to nonprofit organizations as the recipients of subcontracted PSE employees. More than 8,000 PSE participants worked in school districts in the sample jurisdictions. As in the case of other units of local government, the extent of displacement observed in the second round (6 percent) was lower than it was in the first round, apparently because of the large increase in the number of new positions assigned to the schools.

It should be noted that the first observation took place in the summer when school is not in session, while the later observation was made during the school year. In addition, school districts can use large numbers of PSE participants quickly—a highly prized ability when the emphasis of the program is on a rapid increase in enrollment. These individuals are used as hall monitors, crossing guards, maintenance and lunchroom workers, and instructional aides. The timing of the buildup corresponded closely with the school year. Participants in school districts, however, are often given the standard nine-month contract.

STATE AND FEDERAL AGENCIES. State agencies accounted for 4 percent of the PSE positions allotted to the jurisdictions in this study as of December 1977. State agencies are unusual in that they have more sustainment positions than project positions. The probable reason is that state agencies tended to be involved in the PSE program from the outset and so received allocations of sustainment positions. A substantial number of these positions are assigned to state employment services. In return for helping to administer the PSE program with verification, placement, and referral services, state employment services often are allocated PSE participants, and these tend to be sustainment positions.

As in the case of school districts, most PSE participants assigned to state agencies were involved in expanding existing service levels; almost

60 percent were in this category. Four percent of the positions in state agencies were judged to be displacement.

For purposes of analyzing PSE employment effects, state agencies can be divided into two categories. In the first, PSE positions are assigned by the state government directly to state agencies. One such assignment was actually made by a subcommittee of the state legislature. Under such circumstances displacement can easily occur. In the second and larger category, positions are allocated by a local government, and state agencies, like subgovernments or nonprofit organizations, must submit a proposal for positions. Under these circumstances the decision on the allocation of PSE positions is far removed from budget decisions regarding the agency, and the PSE positions involved are far more likely to be used for job creation. This second type of circumstance was also found to apply to federal agencies participating in the PSE program. Federal agencies received a total of 259 positions in the second round from local sponsors. This is less than half of 1 percent of the positions in the sample jurisdictions. In virtually every case the associate judged these positions to have a job creation effect, suggesting that the separation of budget decisions from PSE allocation decisions reduces displacement.

Overall, the degree of displacement was lower than had been anticipated and probably lower than we would have guessed at the outset. This was true even though the sample was overly weighted toward those types of jurisdictions that were thought to be the most likely to use PSE for displacement and fiscal relief. Our method might be inherently conservative. There are a number of local institutional reasons, however, why in retrospect our finding of low displacement might have been anticipated. Unions and civil service systems—both of which would prevent cities from displacing regular workers if the cities tried to do so—are the most obvious. Less obvious is the desire of local officials to avoid providing services with PSE that might have to be continued later out of local funds. Finally, there is the phenomenon of program maintenance, discussed later in this chapter.

Fiscal Effects

The fiscal effects of the PSE program are a separate issue from the program's employment effects, even though the two are related. "Employment effects" refers to how many jobs were created or displaced by

PSE. "Fiscal effects" refers to what eventually happened to the money that went to governments of the PSE program.

There are three kinds of fiscal effects:

—*Expenditure effects* refers to direct spending of funds on the wages of workers holding newly created PSE positions or on administration, or the use of funds released through displacement for expenditures in other areas.

—*Tax effects* stabilize or reduce local taxes. These effects do not put money directly into public employees' hands but do let taxpayers, both individuals and businesses, keep a little more of their incomes.

—*Fund balance effects* occur when a government decides to hold onto any local money it may save by letting PSE support some positions. The government simply builds up a surplus to use later.

Both expenditure effects and tax effects help to stimulate the economy by giving people money to spend; expenditure effects do so directly and through the public sector. We assume, however, that both approaches result in an increase in the federal deficit. If local governments do not use the increase in funds provided by PSE but instead hold them in fund balances, there is no fiscal stimulus and no employment effect either.

The first question is a basic one. Did governments spend their PSE money? The answer is yes. Although as of July 1977 governments were leaving 11 percent of their allocations unspent, that figure dropped to only 3.5 percent by December 1977.

How was the money used? As table 2-5 shows, very little went into idle fund balances. Eighty-six dollars out of 100 had a direct expenditure effect in the public sector, mostly through job creation, while only about 8 dollars out of 100 were used to help stabilize taxes.

Table 2-5 shows that 10 dollars out of 100 were used to administer the PSE program; this is counted as an expenditure effect. This figure probably understates slightly the amount spent for administration, for two reasons. First, this figure counts only federal money spent for salaries of regular administrative employees and excludes PSE participants assigned to the offices that administer PSE. Second, the sample includes some small jurisdictions that do not administer their own PSE programs but instead are essentially subcontractors to larger jurisdictions that handle administrative tasks.

Our conclusion is that most money spent on PSE winds up helping to stimulate the economy directly, and almost all helps to stimulate the economy either directly or indirectly.

Table 2-5. *Employment Distribution of Expenditure and Tax Effects of Public Service Employment*

Effect	Use of funds (*percent*)
Expenditure effects	86
Job creation	75
Administration	10
Displacement	1
Tax effects	8
Tax reduction	*
Tax stabilization	8
Increased fund balances	4
Unallocated	2
Total	100
Addendum:	
Number of governments	38

Source: Data reported by Brookings field associates.
* Less than 0.5 percent; actually 0.4 percent in this tabulation.

The Program Maintenance Effect

The field associates reported that governments used a sizable share of their PSE workers for what we define as program maintenance—that is, keeping public services at their previous level rather than reducing them because of a shortage of local money. We consider program maintenance to be job creation since the number of jobs is greater than it otherwise would be. We do not consider it to be displacement, because displacement means that the city never seriously considered cutting back on services but simply took advantage of federal money to replace local tax efforts. Earlier, associates of the field studies group at Brookings found that many local governments were using revenue sharing funds for the same purpose.

These findings raise two important questions. Did public attitudes toward government spending begin to change in the last half of the 1970s? Were local governments starting to slow down the rate at which they added new workers to the local payrolls, perhaps as a result of voter resistance to higher local taxes?

These questions are important because the answers will help determine whether our estimates of PSE's employment effects are realistic. When the field associates decided that PSE positions were being used to maintain services at their previous levels, they counted those positions in the job creation column rather than the displacement column because they determined that the local government would have abolished those positions unless PSE money had come along at the right time. As noted, one of the grounds on which the associates make this determination is information on changes in demand for public services.

For example, the associate in a large, fiscally pressed city reported:

An examination of the ratio of job creation program maintenance positions to all job creation positions indicates that approximately 25 to 30 percent of the city's creation positions in titles II and VI-sustainment are program maintenance; on the other hand, none of the title VI-project positions are in this category. This indicates that the city clearly treats the programs differently and, beyond the guidelines, is not about to create a possible problem by filling a long-term need with (strictly) short-term money. Virtually all of the positions we classified as maintenance would have been classified as displacement if the fiscal pressure was not so extreme. Title II and VI-sustainment maintenance positions tend to be necessary for high-demand services which would be cut in an emergency, but are now used to maintain services.

By contrast to our method, an econometric or a simple trend study would have determined the rate at which locally funded employment had been increasing in previous years, predicted the increase in subsequent years based on that same rate of increase, and determined whether the actual rate of increase in locally funded employment followed this prediction.[5] If the rate were lower than predicted, the difference would be ascribed to the displacement effect of PSE.

The California voters' passage of Proposition 13 in June 1978, forcing state and local governments to hold down spending increases, was of course a major event that brought media attention to the "taxpayers' revolt." But several researchers have noted that even before that time growth in local public employment had begun to slow. For example, George Peterson of the Urban Institute testified in July 1978:

For the quarter century ending in 1975, local public spending rose year in and

5. "Trend study" refers to extrapolations of employment data as a basis for analyzing the impact of federally aided job programs. Comparing the trend in state and local employment to the change in the level of PSE, Robert D. Reischauer of the Congressional Budget Office estimates that between May 1977 and February 1978, when the PSE program was being expanded, the displacement rate was 42 percent. See Robert D. Reischauer, "The Economy, the Budget, and the Prospects for Urban Aid," in Roy Bahl, ed., *The Fiscal Outlook for Cities* (Syracuse University Press, 1978), p. 104.

year out relative to national product, but during the present economic recovery city expenditures have grown at a much slower rate than national output. Cities suffering economic and population decline have taken the lead in restraining expenditures.[6]

Similarly Michael Borus of Ohio State University and Daniel Hamermesh of Michigan State University reexamined the results of an earlier econometric study of PSE displacement, and William Mirengoff and Lester Rindler did a study for the National Academy of Sciences that used two different approaches to estimating displacement. Both teams of researchers found that equations that allowed for declines in the rate of growth of local employment fit the actual rate of increase better than did equations that predicted a constant rate of increase.[7]

Further evidence of a change in the structure of government employment comes from a close look at figures on the overall number of state and local employees in the nation, excluding employees of public schools. Between October 1970 and 1978 the total rose from 9.9 million to 12.6 million public workers, an average annual rate of increase of 3.2 percent.[8] This figure masks the change that occurred, however. From 1970 to 1975 the average annual rate of increase in state and local noneducation employment was 3.9 percent; from 1975 to 1978 it was only 1.7 percent. This latter figure includes PSE workers as well as regular local and state workers. Even if after 1975 governments began to displace their regular workers with PSE workers, the rate of increase for total employment would have remained the same. Instead, the overall rate of increase dropped, suggesting that governments were cutting back on growth in all public employment.

6. Testimony by George Peterson in *Local Distress, State Surpluses, Proposition 13: Prelude to Fiscal Crisis or New Opportunities?* Hearings before the Subcommittee on the City of the House Committee on Banking, Finance and Urban Affairs and the Joint Economic Committee, 95 Cong. 2 sess. (GPO, 1978), p. 76.

7. Michael Borus and Daniel Hamermesh, "Study of the Net Employment Effects of Public Service Employment: Econometric Analyses," *An Interim Report to the Congress of the National Commission for Manpower Policy: Job Creation through Public Service Employment,* vol. 3: *Commissioned Papers* (NCMP, 1978), pp. 89–149; George Johnson and James Tomola, "The Final Substitution Effect of Alternative Approaches to Public Service Employment Policy," *Journal of Human Resources,* vol. 12 (Winter 1977), pp. 3–26; and William Mirengoff and Lester Rindler, *CETA: Manpower Programs under Local Control* (National Academy of Sciences, 1978), app. B. Borus and Hamermesh used a nonlinear functional form; Mirengoff and Rindler used a log functional form.

8. *Survey of Current Business,* various issues.

We find even more evidence that a simple projection of local and state employment does not reflect changes in the structure of that employment when we look at differences among types of jurisdictions. Between 1970 and 1976 the total number of noneducation public employees in all the large cities in the study sample rose by 4 percent (this figure includes PSE employees). There were big differences, however, in large cities that faced a great deal of fiscal distress and large cities that did not. Total public employment in the latter went up by 13 percent, but dropped by 4 percent in the former. Examples of distressed cities in the sample are Cleveland, where total public employment dropped by 31 percent; Detroit, where it dropped by 8 percent; and Rochester, where it dropped by 27 percent.

As a group, distressed large cities are aided disproportionately under the PSE program because allocations are made largely on the basis of the extent of local unemployment, which tends to be related to the degree of financial stress. The distressed large cities in the sample accounted for 4 percent of all PSE enrollees as of December 1977, but only 1 percent of total state and local employment. This concentration of PSE positions in governments that appear in other respects to be departing from the trend line of city employment adds to the difficulty of conducting econometric or trend studies of the program's employment impact.

We found that small as well as large cities in the sample were cutting back on local employment during the late seventies. For example, the associate who studied one small city reported that the onset of "a period of fiscal austerity" hardened attitudes against the use of PSE positions for displacement purposes.

By 1976, the climate had changed dramatically. Most of the major projects the city council members wanted to achieve had been completed. Taxes had increased substantially and the city was beginning to experience its first real pressure from the suburbanization of business. The 1976 council election revolved around the issue of taxes. Conservatives won two of the three seats up for election. The remaining three members had sensed the attitude of the voters before the 1976 election and the election outcome confirmed their interpretation. A period of fiscal austerity ensued, presided over by the same city manager who had been an expansionist in earlier years. As the next election draws near, economic development and stable taxes are the main concerns of the elected officials. The city manager's policy toward PSE has been consistent with the council's stated intention of not raising taxes. Thus the political-administrative climate is against converting PSE positions to unsubsidized positions.

Implications

The PSE program is supposed to do many things. It is expected to provide large numbers of jobs and to stimulate the economy quickly; to assist persons who had been without jobs for a long time by helping them obtain skills needed to get private jobs, and to provide needed services to the community. Moreover, it is supposed to do these things without contributing to inflation, requiring governments to spend large amounts of money on administration or supervision, or encouraging governments to substitute federally supported positions for locally supported ones.

Two of the questions we sought to answer were whether PSE was resulting in the displacement of many local jobs by federally supported jobs and whether it was helping to stimulate the economy. We found that displacement was not inconsequential but was lower than many persons had thought. Roughly one PSE worker in five was doing a job that would have been filled even if the local government had not received PSE money. We also found that 86 PSE dollars out of 100 were stimulating the economy directly by providing salaries, and another 8 dollars out of 100 were having an indirect stimulus on the economy through the private sector by stabilizing or reducing taxes. Another 4 dollars out of 100 remained in local fund balances and were doing little to stimulate the economy, while we could not classify the effect of the last 2 dollars out of 100 (table 2-5).

Our findings, especially those related to displacement, are at variance with those of some researchers, particularly those who use econometric methods. Our results are consistent, however, with what other researchers have said might be expected from a program of this type and with the results of research on other block grants, such as general revenue sharing.[9] Moreover, the results of econometric studies can vary widely de-

9. Borus and Hamermesh have called PSE a closed-ended categorical grant—closed-ended in that a formula determines how much money goes to each jurisdiction and categorical in that PSE money can be used only to hire labor. Edward Gramlich of the University of Michigan and Harvey Galper of the Treasury Department have suggested that with a closed-ended categorical grant local governments can be expected to actually spend between 65 and 90 percent of the grant money they receive. Gramlich and Galper estimated that a program such as general revenue sharing would cause more substitution than would a program like PSE. The field studies group found through its revenue sharing research that local governments were using 36 percent of those funds for substitution (when program maintenance is not counted

pending on the particular assumptions used and tend to have wide confidence intervals—that is, the actual figures might fall within a broad range of possible analysis outcomes. Our results lie well within the possible range of values reported by these studies.

Several factors are at work to hold down the rate of displacement. We cannot say exactly what the rate would be if each of these factors were removed, but taken together they certainly have an effect. The most important are the following:

—As noted in chapter 1, shortly before our observations Congress tightened the eligibility requirements for the largest part of the program and required governments to place one-half of the new participants in positions related to identifiable temporary projects. These changes were intended to make it more difficult for governments to use PSE positions for displacement; they apparently had the intended effect.

—From the start CETA has contained a "maintenance of effort" clause that bans the use of CETA money for displacement purposes, and the Department of Labor has issued increasingly stringent regulations on this point. Except in the most blatant cases, these regulations are very difficult to enforce. The field associates did report, however, that local government officials generally were at least aware of the ban on displacement.

—Local officials themselves are unlikely to want their government to become dependent on PSE workers for basic services or for continuing fiscal relief, because if Congress were to curtail or eliminate PSE these officials would be faced with a choice of raising taxes or curtailing services to make up for the loss of federal funds, and neither choice is palatable.

—Many local officials in areas facing financial stress are likely to agree with federal officials on the first priority for use of PSE money; to reduce local unemployment as much as possible.

We found that local governments responded to the new eligibility and project requirements in three ways.

---

as substitution). Thus our finding of a 20 percent displacement rate is well within the limits we might theoretically expect based on these studies. See Michael E. Borus and Daniel Hamermesh, "How Much Fiscal Substitution Is There in PSE?" *Industrial Relations Research Association, Proceedings of the Thirty-first Annual Meetings, August 1978* (Chicago: IRRA, 1978), pp. 180–97; Edward Gramlich and Harvey Galper, "State and Local Fiscal Behavior and Federal Grant Policy," *Brookings Papers on Economic Activity, 1:1973,* pp. 15–66; and Nathan, Adams, and Associates, *Revenue Sharing,* p. 310.

First, they developed projects that were different from the government's regular activities or that included activities that otherwise would not have been done. Under the law, however, governments were able to expand activities or to undertake new services that would last more than one year and still call these activities projects. Only one-fourth of the activities that governments undertook with the project portion of the program were really what the associates determined to be new activities that would last one year and then stop.

Second, governments concentrated more on hiring low-income persons and persons who had been unemployed for long periods. We will discuss this effect in detail in the next chapter.

Third, governments subcontracted more positions to outside agencies, especially nonprofit organizations. This increase appeared to be caused not only by the stricter eligibility requirements and the project requirements, but also by a specific requirement in the regulations that one-third of new funding should go to nonprofit organizations, and by the inability of regular government departments to supervise more PSE participants than they already had. Our findings showed less displacement in positions assigned to nonprofit agencies, so the net effect of this change was to reduce displacement.

These results take us back to the theme discussed in the first chapter—the trading off of objectives in the program. Although changes in the program have reduced displacement, what is the effect of these changes on the value of the on-the-job training provided? Do the jobs in nonprofit organizations provide experience that is less likely to lead to unsubsidized employment? Does the use of projects make the program less useful to local governments to the extent that officials may stop paying much attention to it? Are the agencies that can fill slots quickly the ones that provide the best work experience? As the program concentrates on the more disadvantaged, does it enroll people who require more training, supervision, and supportive services than are likely to be available in a program of public employment?

We do not yet know the answers to these questions, but the associates have followed recent developments in PSE and have some idea of the direction in which the program is going. According to a preliminary assessment based on the discussion at a meeting of the associates in October 1979, the result of the changes made by the 1978 reauthorization of the legislation has been that the program now serves an even more disadvantaged population than before, provides jobs that require lower levels of skill or no skills at all and that pay less, and places more workers in nonprofit organizations. The combination of stricter eligibility requirements, lower-wage jobs, and increased use of nonprofit employers probably means there has been less displacement than there was before. But as the program puts more and more emphasis on the structurally unemployed, concern about displacement should lessen. Because Congress has imposed a limit on individual tenure in the program, what was displacement in a countercyclical program may be seen as an effort to stimulate transition to unsubsidized employment in a structural program.

Although the revised program is likely to create more jobs, many of these jobs pay lower wages, require less skill, and in the case of trainees or aides, less direct involvement with the regular local government work force. As a result, persons in these jobs will probably receive less training on the job and fewer of them will move to unsubsidized employment. It is also probable that the value of the services provided by the program participants, particularly as viewed by the local program operators, has been reduced.

CHAPTER THREE

Structural Unemployment

THE PRIMARY emphasis of public service employment at the time of the July and December 1977 field observations was countercyclical job creation. But the structural objective of human capital development was never very far from the surface and reemerged as the dominant PSE goal in the 1978 amended version of the Comprehensive Employment and Training Act. In 1977 the program was expanding rapidly. Most of the participants were in projects, and increasing numbers were placed with nonprofit employers. Because PSE might again be called on to counter recessions, it is important to consider whether a program designed for that purpose can also serve structural objectives.

Three things are necessary for PSE to succeed as a structural program. First, it must target program activities to the appropriate people. Second, it must create training opportunities for those people where they can obtain skills needed to get and hold decent jobs. Third, it must help those people make the transition from subsidized public jobs into unsubsidized jobs. This chapter is an examination of how well PSE has done these three things.

Targeting

Congress has decided that the positions funded by the PSE program should focus on persons who have been unemployed for long periods or who show other evidence of labor market failure. This policy rests on the idea that the structure of today's economy requires workers with skills that enable them to handle increasingly complex information and machinery. People who do not have such skills have trouble finding jobs even when the economy in general is healthy. Different theories suggest different reasons for the disparity of unemployment rates between skilled and unskilled workers, but most economists agree that it exists. Thus the unskilled market may have a pool of "slack" labor, while the skilled market is relatively tight.

Because of the different employment conditions in the skilled and unskilled labor markets, targeting to the unskilled minimizes the danger that jobs created by a public program will push wages up for skilled jobs, or that these jobs will draw skilled workers into the program unless there is excessive overall unemployment. Moreover, such a public employment program will benefit the people for whom it is designed by providing them with job experience. Targeting to those who have low earnings and a history of unemployment therefore is supportable regardless of the state of the economy.

Defining Target Groups

Even when targeting is clearly desirable, phrases such as "structurally unemployed," "unskilled," or "disadvantaged" are not adequate for defining the target group. Nor should the focus simply be on such demographic groups as minorities or women, because not all members of these groups need help. The operational problem is to define the target group so that PSE participants are drawn from a population needing human capital development while assuring that the program does not directly compete with nonsubsidized job opportunities. No targeting criteria can perfectly channel the PSE program to the appropriate group, so it is probably best to focus on indicators of individual labor market failure. In that context it is useful to think of four labor market layers, which can be described (though not precisely defined) as follows:

—The *top layer* consists of persons who hold steady jobs and need no special labor market assistance.

—The *second layer* consists of workers with definite skills who usually hold good jobs but may be laid off in a recession. For example, they may lack seniority or may work in industries that are most sensitive to economic downturns, such as building construction. They typically need short-term relief through income transfers or temporary employment.

—The *third layer* is made up of persons with more long-term problems —those who cannot find satisfactory jobs because they have inadequate skills, face discrimination, or lack information about the labor market. They are likely to have low incomes and to be jobless for long stretches even in prosperous times. These persons need temporary jobs and training and job exposure that will help them move to more stable employment.

—The *bottom layer* consists of persons who lack basic work and communication skills necessary for holding jobs other than temporary unskilled positions. Some have attitudinal or emotional problems, while others may lack the ability to follow directions and work independently. These persons may benefit from a highly structured program of remedial education, training in basic work habits and rudimentary job skills, and counseling, rather than PSE.[1]

The third labor market layer includes those people for whom PSE is an appropriate structural program. Those in the second layer already have greater labor market skills than those likely to be developed in PSE. Those in the lowest layer are not currently prepared to fill the types of positions that are typically created through the program; they need services in addition to employment.

Defining the target group is much easier than reaching it. Targeting restrictions are set by the federal government, but states and localities actually create the jobs and select the participants. In that process there is considerable conflict, since local employing agencies try to hire good workers, while the federal government constrains their choice through restrictions on the jobs and participants.[2]

We cannot determine how well PSE actually reached the target groups in its first few years because data on participants' employment and earnings before they enrolled in the program are incomplete. Program operators did collect data on demographic characteristics; these data suggest that the PSE participants were not much different from the rest of the employed population.

We can gain more information on the characteristics of PSE participants from the Continuous Longitudinal Manpower Survey, an evaluation effort funded by the U.S. Department of Labor. The survey takes annual national samples of enrollees under the Comprehensive Employment and Training Act and collects information on employment, earnings, and family income for the year preceding program participation and for up to three years after program entry. These data, presented in table 3-1, show that many of the participants had experienced a great deal of

1. The use of labor market layers is a way of looking at program target groups. It is not intended as a theory of labor market segmentation but as a way of categorizing the work-related needs of workers and potential labor market participants.
2. The PSE objectives of local governments are explored in chapter 4. The position taken there is that public service provision is an important local government objective and that as a result local governments often attempt to hire the best available workers into PSE positions.

labor market difficulty. For example, considerably more than half of those enrolled in the third quarter of fiscal year 1975 were either unemployed or not in the labor force immediately before program entry, and almost three-fourths of them had earnings of less than $4,000 in the previous year. This is not the expected labor market experience of those in the middle of the skill distribution. Nevertheless, the participant characteristics indicate that the PSE program was not drawing heavily on minorities, youths, or women, the groups considered to experience the most difficulty in finding lasting jobs.

Shortly after PSE began in July 1974 Congress and the administration began to receive reports on the characteristics of participants. Although the program regulations for 1974 required that participants be unemployed or underemployed, the characteristics of enrollees under these rather loose guidelines did not differ substantially from those in the Public Employment Program, which had been criticized for lack of targeting.

As noted in chapter 1, Congress in December 1974 responded to rising unemployment rates by expanding PSE, in part by adding a new PSE component under title VI. The new program was to aim at a more disadvantaged group in PSE by setting lower wage ceilings and requiring that new enrollees had to have been jobless for thirty days before program entry (or fifteen days if the local unemployment rate exceeded 7 percent). With unemployment rates reaching new postwar highs in early 1975, however, eligible participants were abundant. Most of the major labor market areas had unemployment rates in excess of 7 percent, many workers had few job alternatives, and the targeting package did not prove to be very restrictive. In fact, PSE was touted largely as a countercyclical program during this period. The characteristics of participants suggested to many observers that the bulk of PSE participants would find jobs on their own when the economy improved. The program seemed to be targeted to workers in the second layer of the framework described earlier, those who needed only temporary relief.

The character of the program in this period also attracted the attention of government officials. The 1976 *Employment and Training Report of the President* was somewhat apologetic in noting that "the economic situation led to an emphasis on public service employment that temporarily diverted program attention from the basic developmental goal of both titles I and II of CETA."[3] But as the recession waned, another problem

3. *Employment and Training Report of the President* (Government Printing Office, 1976), p. 96.

Table 3-1. *Characteristics of Newly Enrolled Public Service Employment Participants, Selected Periods, 1975, 1976, 1977*

Characteristic	New public service employment participants (percent)			October–December 1977		
	January–March 1975	October–December 1976	July–September 1977	All public service employment	Sustainment positions	Project positions
Age						
Under 22	24	21	22	23	21	22
Over 44	13	12	12	14	12	14
Education						
8 or fewer years	9	6	8	8	9	8
9–11 years	15	15	19	16	12	20
12 years	44	40	36	39	42	35
More than 12 years	32	38	36	37	37	38
Sex						
Male	71	60	64	60	60	61
Female	29	40	36	40	40	39

Race						
White	66	68	62	59	63	55
Black	23	22	29	30	24	37
Hispanic	8	6	7	8	10	6
Other	3	3	2	3	4	3
Unemployed when entered program	49	56	63	64	61	67
Unemployed 6 months out of previous 12	n.a.	30	46	41	37	44
Not in labor force 6 months out of previous 12	n.a.	25	26	27	26	28
Annual family income below $7,500	n.a.	61	72	68	62	75
Earnings in previous year						
Less than $4,000	73	70	86	80	78	82
Less than $1,000	30	42	57	45	40	51

Sources: *Continuous Longitudinal Manpower Survey*, Report 8, prepared by Westat, Inc., for the Office of Program Evaluation, Employment and Training Administration, U.S. Department of Labor (Westat, March 1979), tables 18 and 19 and preliminary unpublished data. Data are from a national sample of new public service employment enrollees; this sample was larger than the Brookings sample.

n.a. = Not available.

became evident—that of getting the layer two workers to move out of PSE when jobs were available in the private sector. The combination of rather loose restrictions on local supplementation to federally paid PSE wages and the lack of any specific limit on the length of time a person could remain in PSE meant that there were some stable, well-paid PSE positions that participants did not have much incentive to leave. Local governments that had taken an interest in the services provided, and thus in the quality of the employees, did not want to push these people out. Although these workers may have obtained considerable job training, they probably did not need it to locate and hold unsubsidized positions.

Because of this situation some policymakers and analysts became concerned about whether a single job creation program could both counter the effects of a recession and combat structural unemployment. A program that accepted anyone who had been jobless just before entering the program would take in two types of persons: those who were only temporarily unemployed and those who were chronically disadvantaged. As we see it, the needs of these two groups differ. Policymakers also asked a second question: Could a program operated by local governments, who presumably wanted to obtain the most productive workers to help provide services, successfully focus on helping low-skilled persons who had been unemployed frequently or for long periods?

Congress tried to provide answers to these questions in 1976. As noted in chapter 1, the reauthorization law passed that year created short-term projects to which some new PSE workers would be assigned and further tightened eligibility requirements to concentrate on persons with low incomes and long histories of unemployment.

The project portion of PSE was roughly equivalent to the expansion of the program, while the previously existing level was called sustainment. Half of the vacancies arising in the sustainment positions were subject to the same participant eligibility requirements as the projects. The net effect was to create a two-tiered program. In effect, Congress was offering local governments a compromise. If the local jurisdictions would operate part of the program under fairly rigid participant restrictions, they could have more latitude in the rest of the program.

The participant data for the last two quarters of calendar year 1977, as shown in table 3-1, suggest that the 1976 targeting provisions moved the PSE program toward those who had experienced more labor market difficulties. These data are for *new* program entrants only, not for all enrollees. From the last quarter of calendar year 1976 to the last quarter of 1977 there was a growing proportion of newly enrolled participants who

Table 3-2. *Public Service Employment Participant Characteristics, Study Sample, by Class of Jurisdiction, Titles II and VI, December 31, 1977*

Characteristic	Public service employment participants (percent)			
	Distressed large cities	Other large cities	Small cities and suburban counties	Rural areas
Male	67	58	61	64
Minority	68	61	24	29
Under 21 years of age	21	19	18	16
Less than 12 years of education	27	14	20	25
Unemployed 15 or more of previous 20 weeks	77	69	58	52
AFDC family member	20	10	6	5
Economically disadvantaged[a]	73	73	73	59
Addendum:				
Number of governments	8	7	11	7

Source: Data reported by Brookings field associates. The percentages in this table are the averages of the means for all jurisdictions in the class. This is the equivalent of treating each jurisdiction as a sample member.

a. At the time these data were gathered an economically disadvantaged person was defined as a single person or member of a family receiving or eligible for welfare payments whose income did not exceed the poverty level or 70 percent of the lower living standard, whichever was higher.

AFDC = Aid to families with dependent children.

in the year before they entered PSE had very low earnings or had been unemployed for long periods, or both. This growth is most evident in the data for October–December 1977. Persons who entered the program in the third and fourth quarters of 1977, especially those assigned to project positions, had lower incomes and had been unemployed for long periods more commonly than had participants in previous years. On the basis of these data, we can conclude that in 1977 the program moved toward helping those with serious structural labor market problems.

The first two rounds of the PSE study focused on the program during this period of change, the last two quarters of calendar year 1977. During the July 1977 observation the program was under pressure to meet the expansion schedule authorized in May of that year as part of the Carter administration's stimulus program. At that time most of the project positions were still to be filled. By the end of the December observation the program had enrolled about 600,000 persons, a figure equal to roughly 80 percent of the eventual peak of 750,000 that was reached in March 1978.

Some of the participant characteristic data gathered in December are shown in table 3-2 by class of jurisdiction and in table 3-3 by type of po-

Table 3-3. *Public Service Employment Participant Characteristics, Study Sample, by Class of Jurisdiction and Type of Position, December 31, 1977*

| | Public service employment participants (percent) | | | | | | | |
| | Distressed large cities | | Other large cities | | Small cities and suburban areas | | Rural areas | |
Characteristic	Sustainment position	Project position	Sustainment position	Project position	Sustainment position	Project position	Sustainment position	Project position
Male	69	65	58	59	58	63	63	62
Minority	61	73	64	60	23	20	26	35
Under 21 years of age	21	19	20	16	16	18	16	17
Less than 12 years of education	28	25	13	14	20	20	21	32
Unemployed 15 or more of previous 20 weeks	57	91	60	77	44	75	47	71
AFDC family	18	29	9	11	6	5	8	4
Economically disadvantaged[a]	63	88	65	80	60	83	58	64
Addendum:								
Number of governments	8	7	7	7	11	10	7	4

Source: Data reported by Brookings field associates. The percentages in this table are the averages of the means for all jurisdictions in the class. This is the equivalent of treating each jurisdiction as a sample member.

a. At the time these data were gathered, an economically disadvantaged person was defined as a single person or member of a family receiving or eligible for welfare payments whose income did not exceed the poverty level or 70 percent of the lower living standard, whichever was higher.

AFDC = Aid to families with dependent children.

sition, that is, project and sustainment positions. Participants in sustainment and project positions were different in several respects, especially in the proportions who had been unemployed fifteen or more of the previous twenty weeks and those who were economically disadvantaged. This difference appears in all classes of jurisdictions, suggesting that the PSE program projects were targeted heavily on the lower layers of the labor market.

The program expanded quickly and shifted its target population, but not without resistance by some local governments. The field associates found that local officials in some areas were reluctant to expand PSE under the stricter eligibility requirements, and many felt they had enough PSE workers. Some officials opposed the 1976 eligibility requirements because they felt that the eligible population was too difficult to supervise and could not adequately perform the kinds of jobs the local government had created, especially given the speed of the expansion in the last half of 1977. A number of officials said their agencies did not have the supervisory personnel, work space, or training capacity to effectively use untrained, disadvantaged employees.

Most associates said they thought the local governments would have problems in trying to expand PSE under the eligibility requirements.

For example, an associate for a large city reported that "local officials are about at the end of the rope in terms of creating new projects and jobs that will work using the current eligibility requirements." Similarly an associate reporting on a rural county commented: "It would be difficult to accommodate an increase in PSE slots. The current targeting on the hard-core unemployed would have to be liberalized considerably."

Such reports introduce another question about targeting: Can it be pushed too far? Between 1975 and 1978 tightened eligibility requirements, along with restrictions on wages and project duration moved the program in the direction of concentrating on those with serious labor market problems. On balance, this is an appropriate shift. But we should not overlook the costs associated with it nor assume that these costs will never outweigh the benefits. It is difficult to assess all the costs because PSE has many objectives; gains and losses may appear on different balance sheets. For example, gains in targeting may be accompanied by losses in the production of local public services. We must talk about how much targeting is appropriate in the context of all the objectives of PSE and of the nature of the bargain between the federal and local governments.

How Far Should Targeting Go?

Local resistance to tighter eligibility requirements seems to stiffen when local officials perceive that they are dipping into what we have called the bottom layer of the labor market. The provision of local public services does not dominate all the decisions about the program in any jurisdiction, but there are few where it does not have some importance. The greater its importance the more the local government is concerned with the performance capability of the PSE participants.

Many of the participants sampled in the field study held jobs similar to those filled by regular employees. They worked directly with permanent jobholders and, as the legislation requires, were paid comparable wages. One indication that the program was valuable to local officials was the extent to which these positions were judged to be program maintenance, meaning that they allowed the continuance of essential services that otherwise would have been curtailed. PSE participants, however, need not be employed in regular government activities to do work that officials feel is important. In fact, the criteria for selection of projects and nonprofit proposals often include the value of the services.

One option open to local governments that are unable to hire good employees for these positions is to refuse to create PSE jobs. As noted, the 1976 targeting regulations led some local officials to resist; it is possible that efforts to push targeting further may threaten the federal-local partnership necessary for a successful program.

Our study has found that the PSE program has moved steadily toward serving long-term unemployed and low-income people, belying the myth that PSE is largely made up of high-paid jobs for highly skilled participants. But they also show that local program operators try to avoid the bottom layer of the labor market. This interplay and balancing of objectives is characteristic of the program. Furthermore, even if PSE is considered only as a structural program, it should focus on those who can make the greatest training gains. Based on the proposition that PSE is not the most appropriate training program for bottom-layer workers and that increased eligibility requirements may threaten local cooperation, we conclude that targeting can go too far. Certainly the most disadvantaged need job experience and exposure to the rules that govern the world of work in ordinary employment. But they may also need constant supervision and basic skill training that the employing agencies at the local level are not willing or able to provide.[4]

Training

Traditionally, Comprehensive Employment and Training Act programs have stressed institutional or formal training for participants. In assessing these programs analysts generally determine the cost of training, duration of enrollment, and skills to be acquired. The chief characteristic of PSE, however, is that it provides *jobs* to the unemployed. To assess the training effectiveness of PSE, we must consider the training impact of the work experience. Through such experience, participants may learn specific job skills and good work habits and improve general skills such as following directions and communicating with fellow workers.

The best way to determine whether such training is effective would be to test the participants' skills before and after they had participated in the program; an alternative would be to compare participants' later earnings with those of a control group. Local governments generally do not give before-and-after skill tests, however, and a comparison with control groups is expensive and requires too much time for immediate policy feedback. The approach followed here is to set up criteria for the most appropriate approach to training in a program like PSE and to assess how well the program meets those criteria.

Factors that Determine Training in Public Service Employment

In judging the effectiveness of training in PSE, we must consider the participants, the nature of the jobs, and the extent of supplementary training.

PARTICIPANTS. The people who are most likely to gain from training in PSE are those in what we have called the third labor market layer. Those in the second layer already have adequate skills; those in the bot-

4. The 1978 amendments to the Comprehensive Employment and Training Act include new participant eligibility requirements, job tenure restrictions, and wage limitations that have focused the 1979–80 PSE program on a more disadvantaged participant group than that enrolled in 1977. While local reactions to these changes are mixed, preliminary field observations show that many local governments have curtailed their PSE involvement, citing the new restrictions as a primary cause.

tom layer need either additional preparation before they can benefit from job experience or more job-related services than most employers are willing to provide.

JOBS. A job that provides useful training is one that requires skills that are related to those used in regular unsubsidized positions. This is most likely to be a job that contributes to a needed service, so that the employer and the supervisor are concerned about the quality of the work. Dead-end jobs that give PSE participants no contact with the regular work force have little relevance to future employment and may even stigmatize participants.

The best training opportunities appear to be in the regular government departments. Managers in these departments are concerned with getting results, and thus are more likely to make some effort to train and supervise their workers. Further, PSE participants in these departments can learn job skills from the regular employees with whom they come in contact. Many local government managers view PSE slots as trainee positions for regular openings that will occur as a result of expansion or turnover. In these instances the "trainees" are actually doing the same thing they will eventually do as regular employees. An associate in a large city reported: "As the Title II workers . . . seem to hold the most responsible positions of all PSE participants . . . they also receive the greatest amount of training."

Because project PSE is restricted to tasks that have a limited and definite duration, participants in these jobs are less likely to move to jobs that use the skills they obtained in PSE. One associate concluded: "Relatively speaking, the least amount of training is provided under Title VI projects. . . . In a project lasting 12 or 18 months the costs of training and time lost is too high to warrant spending any effort in training marginally skilled workers." Another associate had similar reservations about the project employment: "There is a real question about the premise of such project activities as a training ground for future employment in the public sector. The 'project,' while discouraging displacement, has the effect of encouraging irrelevance."

Participants in nonprofit organizations also tend to be involved in specialized activities with little opportunty for direct transition. These participants may receive significant specific training, but most field associates felt that this training is not as applicable to other employment as that obtained by PSE participants in regular government departments. Participants in project positions or in nonprofit organizations may receive significant training, but it is not as likely to be applicable to other employment. As the associate in a suburban county observed: "Many nonprofits cannot provide unsubsidized positions and therefore, even though PSE workers are needed and acceptable, they cannot be transitioned [that is, transferred] into nonexistent positions."

The worst training opportunities occur when local governments treat PSE as a throwaway program for the unskilled and assign participants to cleanup jobs or farm them out to service organizations to work in jobs that have few counterparts in the unsubsidized job market. In a large city, the associate reported: "The general attitude is that with these lower-skilled jobs, a person doesn't need special training beyond the work experience itself. Title VI special project positions should go to the least skilled persons—and of course these positions are the ones that the department or agency has no obligation to train [people for]. . . ." Another associate reported that in one balance-of-state prime sponsor, title VI special projects are almost a disaster. "It is hard to keep them [employees] around at all. We don't give them much training, because it is not worth it. . . ."

Legislative restrictions on PSE in the interest of targeting may also limit the training opportunities. For example, the limit on wages restricts participants to low-paid jobs; as a result, supervisors may expect less from PSE workers, and regular employees may feel threatened by "cheap labor" and may refuse to cooperate in training participants.

SUPPLEMENTARY TRAINING. Some persons who have had serious problems in finding and keeping jobs in the regular labor market may need some help in addition to what they learn on the job. This help may take the form of extra supervision, some classroom skill training, or job counseling. But these supplementary activities should not be the chief form of training; participants are most likely to obtain the skills they need by working on the job. Where extensive training is needed before employment, it should be done through some program other than PSE.

Does Public Service Employment Fulfill Its Training Potential?

If we judge PSE on the criteria listed above, we can conclude that it has a great potential for training participants. The participant data suggest that most local jurisdictions are now enrolling more participants from the group that can benefit from PSE on-the-job training—those in what we call the third layer of the job market—rather than from those who already have significant job skills. A large portion of PSE jobs are in departments and functional areas where local governments are committed to providing services. Just because PSE has potential for offering training, however, does not mean that it fulfills that potential. How well are participants' training needs matched with training opportunities PSE programs offer?

Reports from our field associates reveal a wide disparity in the attention to training among the jurisdictions in our sample. Most jurisdictions had no discernible training policy. So little supplementary training was offered that, overall, it was judged to be insignificant.

In fact, in the vast majority of the sample jurisdictions the training of PSE participants was not a major concern of those administering the program. While this is an important finding, considerable informal training on the job occurred even in jurisdictions where it was not an important objective.

Some of the best training opportunities were in jurisdictions that had both fiscal problems and a large population of persons with chronic labor market difficulties, as shown by high unemployment rates and large numbers of persons with low incomes. Due to extreme fiscal pressure, local officials in these jurisdictions used PSE positions for essential services, thereby creating "real" jobs within regular departments; meanwhile the heavy concentration of unemployed and low-income persons in the program forced managers to deal with the training needs of participants.

The training opportunities in these jurisdictions occur precisely because of the primacy of government service production as a local PSE objective.

From one large city an associate gave this report:

Where governmental units employ additional people they behave in a predictable and understandable fashion. Within the enforceable constraints imposed by the law, they hire the best people for the jobs. When they design the job, no prior thought is given to the needs of the persons who may be available for work at the allowable wage. Consequently, the two most frequent criticisms of PSE are that workers are not qualified for the positions that are open in the local area and that the allowable wage is too low. These are two sides of the same complaint and reflect a concern with the job to be done rather than the worker.

Another associate described a similar attitude on the part of local program officials in a large city: "PSE participants are selected to meet the demands of the jobs; jobs are not developed to reflect the skill level or characteristics of eligible participants. This situation is true for 99 percent of the matching of jobs and clients."

This extensive attention to the jobs rather than to the participants is consistent with the lack of training policy and supplementary training. The training gains were often judged to be substantial in these areas, however, because training was frequently required to improve the workers' performance. In many jurisdictions these gains occur as a result of the tension between federal and local objectives. The federal mandate to enroll the long-term unemployed directs the program to those with training needs, while the local interest in public services creates the jobs from which training gains are possible.

The opportunities for on-the-job training will decline if the targeting objectives are bypassed. Some jurisdictions successfully avoided enrolling the people who can most benefit from PSE, even under quite stringent eligibility requirements. Others fired or pushed out the participants who could not perform well on the job. Still others had two-tiered programs where the good jobs were reserved for the participants who were most job ready and the participants most in need of training were shunted off to jobs with little training potential. In spite of these cases, however, the training picture in areas with no training policy and little concern for the training needs of participants were better served than it seemed at first glance. The training is just as effective when it is done because the supervisor is concerned with output as it is when it occurs because someone is concerned with participant needs.

In other cases the local governments served the appropriate target population but did not create jobs with training potential. Local officials in these jurisdictions saw PSE as simply another federal relief program for the poor. The PSE jobs required little skill and provided little opportunity.

The following excerpt from an associate's report vividly portrays just such a situation:

The extent of PSE training is very limited and consists of nothing more than a brief orientation session. In fact, one of the most common complaints expressed by city department personnel administrators is that the program provides for no training. The hard core unemployed are suddenly plunged into the job setting with very little counseling other than the brief discussion of work habits, etiquette expectations, etc., that occurs between the PSE applicant and the counselor for the city department in which the applicant is placed. These sessions usually last about 15–30 minutes. There is virtually no supervision or on-the-job training. One personnel administrator summed up the situation as follows: "The program started out as a good idea—a way to train people. However, the way it's being done is, 'Here's a body. Put it to work doing anything you need done.' They don't even check to see if the person is doing the work his job description says he should be doing. We can use them any way we want. They wouldn't know, or care."

According to the associates some local officials felt that the restrictions on eligibility, wages, and duration of employment were so constraining that it was not fruitful to use PSE participants in regular functional activities. These officials developed maintenance and cleanup projects and special community services that offered little training.

Even within a single jurisdiction practices vary among departments and employers. Top local officials may set guidelines and objectives, but they seldom make the actual hiring decisions or take a direct role in creating jobs. As an associate from one large city reported: "There is built-in tension between the manpower agency, which wants the positions designed to fit eligible participants, and hiring agencies, which want participants to meet the demands of the positions." Another said that "PSE positions are most likely to be designed to fit the characteristics of eligible participants in title VI special projects, city departments, and departments and agencies with experience in participating in federal jobs programs."

To sum up, training situations in PSE vary widely among and within jurisdictions. The targeting restrictions have promoted training in most areas by pushing jurisdictions to enroll those with training needs, although in some cases the push may have gone so far that cities stop creating jobs with valuable training content. It is clear that the interplay of participant needs and job content must be given careful attention in designs to improve training output and that on-the-job training provides the most significant gains from a job creation program.

Transition

In considering how well PSE participants make the transition from subsidized to unsubsidized jobs, one must also consider what kind of person enters PSE and what economic conditions prevail in the jurisdictions that use the greatest numbers of PSE participants. Moving PSE participants to jobs in the private market would be easy if those participants already had job skills when they entered the program. Similarly, transition would be easy if the local economy were healthy and plenty of private jobs were available. But PSE is aimed at persons who lack marketable job skills and at areas with high rates of unemployment. If transition were easy, PSE would not be needed.

At the time of the second field observation, the federal regulations for title II encouraged local governments to try to place half of all participants in unsubsidized employment. The title VI regulations also set such a goal, adding that it should be met "to the extent feasible." Because most jurisdictions target PSE to the long-term unemployed, a goal of placing most participants directly into unsubsidized positions seems ambitious, especially in the distressed areas. Few jurisdictions met this goal. Most of the jurisdictions we studied did not set specific transition goals.

In a major metropolitan city the associate noted:

The transition to unsubsidized employment has not been good. . . . There seems to have been created a permanent cadre of PSE-subsidized individuals. Little effort is made to place these employees into unsubsidized jobs because there is no cost to failure and no incentive to succeed. Transition is not the concern of local officials; their concern is securing more PSE positions (the countercyclical mentality). There are not significant differences by title.

Local officials appeared to be unsure about the local employment possibilities and the future state of the economy. In addition, some local officials noted that they were unable to keep track of participants after they left the program and thus could not adequately report on placements. Some were concerned that confirmed placement rates always give the minimum transition rate and understate program success.

Although few jurisdictions had specific transition policies, this does not mean they had no interest in what happened to participants after they left the program. In fact, supervisors often gave PSE participants paid time to look for regular jobs. Managers also frequently regarded PSE participants as candidates for vacant positions that occur in the department or agency where they are employed.

For example, the associate in one large city reported:

There is no policy within the city with regard to a particular rate of transition. Officials pay lip service to the principle and provide good anecdotes of successful transition, but they are unable to delineate a particular transition policy or to provide good data to help us understand current transition rates. It should also be noted that the city does encourage transition and provides ample notice of vacancies in permanent positions as well as ongoing counseling for PSE employees to apply for and be tested for regular city positions.

Local officials' greatest concern about transition from PSE to unsubsidized employment is that it does not entirely depend on how well the program is operated. Even though targeting may be appropriate and some training accomplished, transition may be difficult.

Each jurisdiction had a number of reasons for low transition rates. Among the most frequently cited are that state and local governments had imposed general hiring limits on agencies; participants lacked private-sector connections, and private employers resisted hiring those whose past employment record in the private sector indicated an inability to hold a job; participants failed to pass civil service or other employee examinations; and the region had few job vacancies. None of these reasons indicates a direct failure of the program to target or train.

Some of the more concerned local officials made vigorous transition efforts. An associate in a large city commented: "Attempts to maximize transition include efforts to improve relations with Employment Security, efforts to improve the PSE image with local firms . . . and with local labor leaders, and a policy of hiring only PSE participants for regular entry-level positions in city government."

Another city planned to make transition and training a crucial factor in awarding contracts, to closely monitor transition efforts, and to withdraw PSE slots from city agencies that did not meet training and transition objectives.

Thus transition, the last step in the successful sequence of structural policy, is the most difficult to attain. The structural program aimed at training the unskilled can only succeed if there are jobs at the end of the process. That step requires a healthy economy and the removal of some hiring restrictions, conditions that neither the participants nor program operators can bring about. Program operators do, however, have the power to emphasize the potential placement of participants and to train with that end in mind.

Implications and Conclusions

In this chapter we have looked at PSE as a structural program by considering its targeting, training, and transition potential. Conclusive judgments about the success of the actual operating program are difficult to make for several reasons, including the fact that some of the factors that may indicate success are beyond the control of the program operators. For example, program operators usually must simply assume that participants are trainable and that private-sector jobs will be available for those who complete the program. Another difficulty in assessing the success of PSE is that, as noted several times in this volume, it is a program with multiple and sometimes conflicting objectives. PSE could undoubtedly be a better structural program if all other goals were sacrificed. General conclusions about training and transition are difficult to draw because the program differs among areas and program segments and because it has changed in size and purpose several times in the past half decade.

In the absence of specific indicators of success, we have tried to consider the conditions under which PSE is most likely to offer long-term labor market gains to participants and have compared the actual program to that ideal. In doing so we have given attention to the interaction of structural and other program objectives, taking into account some of the political factors that shape the eventual outcome. A major theme of the field study of PSE is that the PSE program is a policy bargain among conflicting interests. Nowhere is that more evident than in the analysis of PSE as a structural policy.

One of the most interesting conclusions reached here is that the tension between conflicting interests may strengthen certain aspects of PSE as a job-training program. For instance, federal officials want PSE to focus on the most disadvantaged, while local officials want to use PSE participants to provide useful public services. The result in some areas has been that the program enrolls people with real labor market difficulties, though not necessarily those at the bottom of the labor market ladder, and then assigns them to jobs in regular government departments. As noted, it is just those departments that offer the greatest training and transition potential. Even though the local governments must limit PSE workers to low-wage jobs, this result shows that a workable compromise has been reached that has considerable promise as an element of structural policy.

Of course, not all jurisdictions, nor all program components within jurisdictions, have reached such a productive compromise. Some areas use PSE funds without generating the training opportunities that will help participants find permanent employment. That can occur either because the jurisdiction hires persons who do not require training or because the jobs require little skill and offer little training, or both.

In any case the PSE program constantly responds to changes in federal restrictions and priorities as well as to changes in local conditions. These changes may improve or damage PSE as structural policy. The problem is that because a successful structural program depends on so many interrelated features, any particular change may not have the intended effects. Specifically, the field study shows that federal restriction on wages, duration of program enrollment, and participant eligibility may harm PSE's ability to combat structural unemployment. If federal rules require governments to pay PSE participants less than regular government workers, the local jurisdictions may not be able to create jobs with a valuable training component. These wage limits, in combination with stringent participant eligibility requirements, could make PSE more of a work relief program where the skills used on the job bear little relevance to unsubsidized employment. In that case training and transition would be sacrificed for targeting.

The workability of PSE as structural policy depends on the objectives and incentives of the federal government, local jurisdictions, and participants. These are shaped and constrained by the law, the state of the economy, local institutions, and some strictly political concerns. Because the process is so complex, and because the program differs from place to place and from time to time, we must be cautious in making conclusions about the success or failure of PSE. Nevertheless, the research results indicate that for many jurisdictions the balancing of interests has resulted in a targeted structural program with considerable potential.

CHAPTER FOUR

The Provision of Public Services

Most previous studies of public service employment have focused on the countercyclical and structural policy implications of the program. Yet the services provided by the hundreds of thousands of PSE participants are of considerable consequence to the states and localities where they work. This chapter is a discussion of the types of services provided and the importance of this aspect of the program to local officials. We find that the provision of services is not only an important objective of PSE, but that it also has implications for the program as countercyclical and structural policy.

The analysis of services provided through PSE is critical to our view of how the program functions. When seen as a federal-local transaction, PSE clearly depends on the cooperation of both parties. That cooperation is assured when both parties move toward meeting some set of accepted goals. To the extent that local governments are more interested than the federal government in the services that PSE participants provide, these services are a key element in understanding how the program is implemented. For example, we noted in the previous chapter that targeting PSE positions to the most disadvantaged is resisted by some local governments because of local attention to the quality of employees and the value of the services they provide.

We have maintained that targeting is important to the success of PSE as countercyclical and structural policy and that the ability to target is limited by local cooperation. If these premises are valid, then the role of public service provision in forming the PSE program is a vital one.

Our field study strongly confirms this point. Because services are an important PSE objective, we asked several questions about services. For example, to the extent that PSE creates new jobs, what services do the new jobholders provide and why are these services important to local communities? Another line of questioning deals with compatibility among PSE objectives. Is local attention to services consistent with a program designed to alleviate the labor market difficulties of the disadvantaged? Do the federal constraints on the program give local governments enough latitude to operate the kind of program they are satisfied with? How are the local institutions, such as public employee unions and personnel systems, treated in the creation of local government jobs? In discussing these questions we draw heavily on the reports from the network of on-site observers.

Public Service Provision as a Local Objective

PSE grants usually constitute a substantial increase in local government funds. Although local governments may be tempted to use these funds to provide local fiscal relief (discussed in chapter 2), we found that governments used only a small portion of the funds for this purpose. The major portion of the grants was used to expand local services.

In both rounds of the field study the local interest in the quality of those services was directly evident from the program designs of local governments, which stressed the public service output. Such interest is also shown in the local attention to the quality of the participants. In approximately three-fourths of the sample jurisdictions, the associates felt that participants were selected to meet the demands of the jobs created, rather than the jobs being designed to meet the needs of the participants. In most jurisdictions the sequence of PSE employment begins when the local officials select positions and projects they think are most valuable to the community, often with the counsel of community-based advisory groups. The governments then list or advertise the positions, and government managers select the most qualified persons from among the eligible applicants. In this process, the interest in public services shapes both the types of jobs created and the types of participants hired.

What Services Are Provided?

The most direct way to assess the kinds of services provided is to look at what participants are doing, and one of the best means to do this is to examine how participants are distributed among different types of services. The field associates found PSE participants in almost all kinds of government departments and agencies as well as in hundreds of nonprofit organizations. Within local governments the distribution of PSE participants across service types is quite similar to the distribution of all jobs in services regularly provided by those governments.

The following series of excerpts from the reports of associates indicates the variety of services that are provided.

In the early days of PSE the positions were deployed to stabilize primary services (i.e., public works, parks, real property) but the new project money is being used for more social services. Child care, drug treatment, and elderly care are representative of this branching out into variable services.

* * *

Some educational services would be cut back without PSE. In the school district we find teachers, teacher's aides, and clerical workers in PSE slots. At the community college, PSE participants run special programs in drama, music, and vocational training. At the university, many PSE participants are research aides or clerical workers.

* * *

Brush clearing, park and recreation area improvement, record keeping, library services, and social services requiring extensive client contact have all been visibly improved by local PSE employment.

* * *

Two PSE projects have served as successful pilots which may lead to regional programs. One is a cancer screening and education program. Eleven other municipalities have shown an interest in sharing in this project. Some qualified personnel have been trained through this project.

* * *

PSE has been a stimulus for the creation of many nonprofit organizations in the county which now provide residents with a migrant health center, homemaker services, crisis intervention centers, and numerous other cultural and social service programs.

Distribution of PSE Participants by Functional Area

Table 4-1 shows the distribution of participants by category of service or functional area for the field study jurisdictions in both July and December 1977. Both observations are shown here because there was a rapid buildup in PSE, especially in the projects, in the interim. The PSE data are presented separately for distressed large cities, other large cities, small cities and suburban counties, and rural areas. Also shown is the distribution of regular government positions in 1976 for major cities and counties in the United States. Functional areas are grouped into the following general categories:

Primary service. These include protective services, public works, utili-

Table 4-1. *Distribution of Public Service Employment Participants, Sample Jurisdictions, by Functional Area and Class of Jurisdiction, July and December 1977, and Regular Government Positions in Major Cities and Counties, 1976*

Percent

| Functional area | Public service employment participants | | | | | | | | Regular government positions, major cities and counties, 1976 |
| | Distressed large cities | | Other large cities | | Small cities and suburban counties | | Rural areas | | |
	July	December	July	December	July	December	July	December	
Primary services	56	44	47	37	30	49	40	54	51
Protective services	17	10	12	5	8	8	9	24	21
Public works	29	11	11	16	12	17	17	16	8
Utilities and sanitation	3	14	11	9	4	10	3	3	10
General administration	7	9	13	7	6	15	11	11	12
Social and cultural services	18	26	19	32	29	25	20	21	17
Social services	13	15	11	22	26	16	13	15	5
Health	4	8	4	4	1	8	4	5	12
Culture and arts	1	3	4	6	2	1	3	1	n.a.
Parks and recreation	15	17	14	8	12	11	4	14	5
Education	8	8	10	19	16	14	19	12	21
Miscellaneous	3	5	8	5	14	2	19	. . .	8

Sources: Field data reported by Brookings field associates, and U.S. Bureau of the Census, *Public Employment in 1976*, Ser. GE76-No. 1 (Government Printing Office, 1977). U.S. Census Bureau functional areas were changed slightly to provide greater comparability with field data. Figures are rounded.

n.a. = Not available.

ties and sanitation, and general administration. This category roughly parallels the U.S. Census Bureau's definition of "common functions" for municipalities. Primary services are almost always provided by local governments and are funded chiefly from local revenues.

Social and cultural services. These services include health care, services for the elderly, museums, and theaters. Although most cities and counties provide some of these services, the levels and combinations of services vary considerably. In most areas the state and federal governments are more involved in the funding and administration of these services than they are in primary services.

Parks and recreation. For purposes of the PSE program this has been separately classified, even though the Census Bureau counts it as a common function. Many of the PSE positions in this classification are used for services that are more like recreational and social services than primary services.

Education. Education is classified separately because it is generally provided by school districts, which often have a high degree of independence from the local government, both in financing and administration.

The July field data and the data for regular government positions show very similar patterns, particularly in the heavy emphasis on primary services. These are the services most often performed by local governments. Most of the projects were implemented between July and December; a comparison of the two periods shows a significant decline in the large cities in the percentage of participants in the primary services. This drop is undoubtedly due to federal restrictions on projects. These restrictions included requirements that projects last one year or less and that they enroll participants with greater labor market difficulties. As a result the project positions were not so easily used in slots that were like regular government jobs. Even so, the number of participants in primary services did not go down over the period; instead, the program growth was merely concentrated in other areas.

The picture is more complicated for the smaller sample jurisdictions, where the percentage of participants in primary services appears to have increased between July and December 1977. The high percentage of unassigned positions in the earlier period, however, makes it difficult to be certain whether any change occurred in the provision of primary services in these areas.

On the whole the project expansion apparently accomplished the intended purposes of limiting displacement and targeting the program to

Table 4-2. *Distribution of Public Service Employment Participants, Sample Jurisdictions, by Functional Area, Type of Position, and Class of Jurisdiction, December 1977*

	Distressed large cities		Public service employment participants (percent) Other large cities		Small cities and suburban counties		Rural areas	
Functional area	Sustainment position	Project position	Sustainment position	Project position	Sustainment position	Project position	Sustainment position	Project position
Primary services	48	35	47	29	56	45	55	43
Protective services	10	11	7	2	9	9	25	2
Public works	10	9	20	14	17	17	15	24
Utilities and sanitation	17	7	9	11	12	8	4	1
General administration	11	8	11	2	18	11	11	16
Social and cultural services	24	33	22	41	21	27	20	22
Social services	10	23	15	29	15	15	14	21
Health	8	7	4	3	5	10	5	1
Culture and arts	6	3	3	9	1	2	1	...
Parks and recreation	19	13	10	6	12	9	11	25
Education	6	10	15	19	10	17	13	10
Miscelleaneous	3	9	6	5	1	1	1	...

Source: Data reported by Brookings field associates.

more disadvantaged participants, but it also had the unintended effect of altering the mix of public services. Some local officials saw the project limitations as a serious threat to local autonomy and a blow to PSE as a valuable local resource. The differences in functional area distribution between the project and sustainment portions of the program are quite large (see table 4-2). At the time of the December observation Congress had not yet set a limit on the length of time a participant could be enrolled in the sustainment positions, and there was considerably more flexibility in choosing participants for sustainment positions than in choosing participants for project positions. Consequently governments used a larger proportion of sustainment positions for primary services. Thus in the part of the program over which they had greatest control, local governments used PSE most often to provide services that are traditionally more important to them.

The sample data also show the relationship between fiscal conditions and the types of services provided. The discussion in chapter 2 showed that jurisdictions facing extreme fiscal pressure were most likely to use PSE for combined program maintenance and displacement activities. This kind of use could show up in a concentration of program positions in those functional areas that officials regard as most critical.

The field study results do not show any clear pattern of services corresponding to different degrees of fiscal pressure, however. For the large cities the differences in functional area distribution are not great, although cities under extreme fiscal pressure devoted more of their positions to protective services and fewer to social services.[1] In the smaller jurisdictions the differences are much greater; areas where the fiscal pressure was great put more emphasis on primary services. But the number of jurisdictions in this category was too small for us to put much emphasis on this finding. The effects of fiscal pressure on the types of services delivered do not appear strong and seem to differ by type of jurisdictions. The effects do tend, however, to be in the expected direction: more emphasis on primary services where fiscal pressures are greater.

Different types of employers use PSE participants for different types of functions. As table 4-3 shows, the majority of participants who work directly for the sample governments are employed in the primary services. The same is true of participants who work for other local governments

1. The functional area distribution of PSE participants in large jurisdictions is of the sampled agencies, not all agencies. This may be one reason why fiscal pressure did not show a more consistent effect on service mix.

Table 4-3. *Distribution of Public Service Employment Participants, Sample Jurisdictions, by Functional Area, Employing Agency, and Class of Jurisdiction, Titles II and VI, December 1977*

Public service employment participants (percent)

Functional area	Large cities				Small cities, suburban and rural areas			
	Principal government	*School district*	*Other local governments*	*Nonprofit organizations*	*Principal government*	*School district*	*Other local governments*	*Nonprofit organizations*
Primary services	58	...	52	6	67	...	60	5
Protective services	10	...	7	*	20	...	15	1
Public works	22	...	36	1	20	...	11	3
Utilities and sanitation	14	...	4	5	7	...	9	*
General administration	12	...	5	*	20	...	25	1
Social and cultural services	17	...	33	71	18	1	19	86
Social services	8	...	29	51	11	...	16	69
Health	6	...	4	7	6	1	2	14
Culture and arts	3	...	...	13	1	...	1	3
Parks and recreation	19	1	3	6	14	...	11	3
Education	*	99	12	6	1	99	10	5
Miscellaneous	6	...	1	10	1	...	1	1
Addendum:								
Number of governments	16	14	7	14	17	10	11	12

Source: Data reported by Brookings field associates. The total number of positions allotted to state and federal agencies was too small to be reported here.
Note: The figures in this table are averages, by sample jurisdiction, for those governments where data on the employing agency are complete.
* Less than 0.5 percent total.

with whom the sample jurisdictions have subcontracting arrangements. (This concentration is greater than that of regular workers as shown in table 4-1.) By contrast, most participants assigned to nonprofit organizations work in social and cultural services.

Local governments are especially likely to use PSE for public works, reflecting the tendency to use PSE for repair and construction work that may otherwise be postponed. Governments using PSE workers for such purposes get needed work done and at the same time avoid the danger that a future cut in PSE funding might disrupt operating programs. Examples of public works undertaken by PSE employees include repair and maintenance of airports, streets, and harbors; beautification of buildings and highways; and housing improvements.

The concentration on social and cultural services in nonprofit organizations is not surprising, since many of the nonprofit organizations in the country are devoted to social and cultural activities. Some of these organizations are virtually creatures of PSE, arising in direct response to the availability of funds and positions.

Occupations of PSE Participants

Functional area data show what kinds of services PSE workers provide, but the occupational distribution of participants provides more information about what they actually do. That is, even if we know that a large portion of participants are engaged in public works, we do not know whether they are engineers, laborers, or clerks.

Table 4-4 compares the national distribution of all employed persons by occupation with that of sample jurisdiction PSE participants. The latter are shown to be more likely to be in the low-skilled occupations. Tables 4-5 and 4-6 indicate that the jobs in the PSE program are mostly in the categories of laborer, service, clerical, and paraprofessional. Generally these are the types of jobs that require the least skill and pay the least money.

There is little difference from one class of jurisdiction to another in the distribution of occupational categories. The patterns are similar even for distressed large cities and rural areas, which are quite different in other respects. The percentage of PSE participants in the lower-pay occupations is slightly greater for the project positions than for the sustainment positions.

Table 4-4. *Distribution of Public Service Employment Participants, Sample Jurisdictions, by Occupation and Class of Jurisdiction, December 1977, and All U.S. Employees, 1976*

Percent

	Public service employment participants				
Occupation	Distressed large cities	Other large cities	Small cities and suburban areas	Rural areas	All U.S. employees
Managerial	1	1	1	2	12[a]
Administrative	3	4	6	7	0
Professional	7	8	6	4	17[b]
Paraprofessional	9	14	8	7	n.a.
Technical	1	1	3	1	0
Technician	3	3	5	3	n.a.
Clerical	13	19	22	24	20
Craft	7	2	3	2	14
Operative	4	2	4	10	17
Laborer	35	30	35	27	6
Service	17	16	7	13	14
Addendum: Number of governments	8	8	11	7	...

Sources: Data reported by Brookings field associates; and U.S. Department of Labor, Bureau of Labor Statistics, *Handbook of Labor Statistics, 1977*, Bulletin 1966 (Government Printing Office, 1977), table 18, p. 61. Excluded are sales workers, private household workers, farmers, farm laborers, farm managers, and farm supervisors.

a. Includes both managerial and administrative occupations.
b. Includes both professional and technical occupations.
n.a. = Not available.

Even when one arrays the occupational data by type of employing agency it is seen that a majority of the participants employed by each type are in the lower-pay occupational categories. School districts and nonprofit organizations employ relatively high proportions of paraprofessionals, perhaps because of the large number of trainee and aide positions. Local governments have the highest percentage of laborers. But regardless of how the data are displayed—by class of jurisdiction, program segment, or employing agency—the bulk of the participants are in the occupations requiring the least skill.

The Value of Public Service Employment Services

Because providing services is an objective that shapes the PSE program, it is important to ask whether these services are really valuable to

Table 4-5. *Distribution of Public Service Employment Participants, Sample Jurisdictions, by Occupation, Class of Jurisdiction, and Type of Position, December 1977*

| | Public service employment participants (percent) | | | | | | | |
| | Distressed large cities | | Other large cities | | Small cities and suburban counties | | Rural areas | |
Occupation	Sustainment positions	Project positions	Sustainment positions	Project positions	Sustainment positions	Project positions	Sustainment positions	Project positions
Managerial	*	3	1	*	2	*	2	1
Administrative	5	3	4	4	7	4	7	1
Professional	11	5	7	9	6	5	4	3
Paraprofessional	6	11	11	15	8	8	8	5
Technical	1	*	1	1	2	5	*	2
Technician	6	1	2	4	4	7	4	1
Clerical	15	11	25	12	27	19	25	28
Craft	4	9	1	3	5	2	2	4
Operative	5	4	4	2	4	4	10	3
Laborer	33	32	28	33	27	39	25	43
Service	13	21	15	16	8	6	13	8
Addendum:								
Number of governments	8	7	8	8	11	10	7	4

Source: Data reported by Brookings field associates.
* Less than 0.5 percent of the total.

Table 4-6. *Distribution of Public Service Employment Participants, Sample Jurisdictions, by Occupation, Employing Agency, and Class of Jurisdiction, Titles II and VI, December 1977*

	Public service employment participants (percent)							
	Large cities				Small cities, suburban and rural areas			
Occupation	*Principal government*	*School district*	*Other local governments*	*Nonprofit organizations*	*Principal government*	*School district*	*Other local governments*	*Nonprofit organizations*
Managerial	1	0	2	2	1	0	1	1
Administrative	4	0	5	8	7	1	3	8
Professional	6	10	11	11	3	6	11	8
Paraprofessional	5	30	15	16	2	16	4	21
Technical	1	0	1	1	2	1	1	1
Technician	4	1	2	2	4	3	2	3
Clerical	15	19	19	15	26	25	30	22
Craft	4	4	2	8	2	3	9	3
Operative	5	0	2	1	10	6	5	6
Laborer	43	9	24	20	32	23	22	13
Service	14	27	16	17	13	17	11	14
Addendum:								
Number of governments	16	14	7	16	17	10	11	12

Source: Data provided by Brookings field associates. Figures are rounded.

the community. The previous section revealed how local governments tend to use PSE positions in the primary services and that a majority of all participants are in occupations requiring the least skill. The value of the output, however, depends on how much is produced and whether the services meet community needs.

Quantity of PSE Services

The field study associates compared the productivity of PSE participants with that of regular government workers. In a majority of the sample areas PSE participants were reported to be about as effective as regular employees working in similar jobs. In a few cases associates reported that the program participants were less effective because the eligibility requirements forced the local jurisdictions to hire untrained workers. In other instances, however, managers thought PSE participants were actually superior, sometimes because they had the added incentive of trying to secure regular employment. Generally PSE employees appeared to carry out their assigned duties in an acceptable way. While this is not a startling conclusion, given what we know about the functional area and occupational distribution of participants, it presents a picture somewhat different from that often developed in the popular press—a picture of PSE as an income transfer program for people who are unwilling to actively seek regular employment.

Community Demand for PSE Services

If people express demands for government goods as they do for private goods—that is, if they order their preferences and buy first those items that yield the greatest satisfaction—then the services provided through PSE are likely to be of less average value than those funded by locally raised revenues. Otherwise taxpayers would have provided the additional services before PSE funding was available. The results of the field study provide no compelling evidence to contradict this hypothesis. Under certain conditions, however, PSE services are highly valued by the community, perhaps only slightly less than those provided out of local funds. We saw three types of cases where PSE services were very important in several of the sample jurisdictions.

First, we found that in many jurisdictions a large share of PSE positions were used for program maintenance. These jurisdictions—often fiscally distressed cities where the tax base is declining—were unable to fund the existing level of services without relying on PSE. Such cities need greater protective services, sanitation, education, and parks and recreation. The fact that the community is not now paying for these services may be largely due to an inability to pay rather than to a judgment that the services are not important. The potential value of PSE-funded services in such areas appears quite high. That is not to say that these services are as highly valued as those funded from local revenues in these localities. But in fiscally distressed communities PSE may be used to provide services that *are* funded out of local revenues in more affluent communities. The associate in a large fiscally distressed city reported: "PSE has enabled the city to maintain (and in some cases, improve) the level of services provided to citizens. . . . Most notable have been protective, health, and sanitation services. Without PSE, the level of services in these and other areas would surely have deteriorated further."

Second, PSE provides highly valued services where "absorption" occurs as a result of a "demonstration effect," that is, a PSE service that was originally not considered to be a permanent activity becomes so important that it would be maintained out of regular government funds if PSE were eliminated. In one example of absorption, an associate reported: "There is little doubt that, from the point of view of the city council members and city administrators, a portion of the PSE services could not now be eliminated—absorption at some rate is the inevitable consequence of successful PSE." Absorption occurred in diverse activities, including public safety, library services to the aged, sanitation, and public works.

The following examples from the reports of the associates may help to clarify how the absorption of PSE services actually occurs.

At the time the PSE sign painter was employed it was felt that the position would be only temporary. However, the work performed proved to be of such utility and quality that the city concluded it had a need which it had not previously recognized and decided to retain the position permanently.

*   *   *

The 100 Spanish-speaking public safety aides are all PSE; there are no city-funded positions of that type to which they can make the transition, although some do become police officers. These aides are now probably indispensable and most would be hired on city funds if PSE were terminated. . . . It is not clear however, that the city would raise taxes to pay for PSE personnel who have become indispensable. It is more likely that the city would find money by cutting back on services with lesser priority.

*   *   *

So far, we have moved three CETA [Comprehensive Employment and Training Act] employees into regular positions. One was a newly created position of dispatcher which was a direct result of CETA funding. The citizens of the town were able to see that this service is needed.

Absorption can be seen as induced demand and, depending on its extent, may be an important consequence of PSE. But at the time of the second observation in December 1977 the rate of absorption was probably quite low. Most associates reported that it was not very important in their jurisdictions and none indicated that a majority of the PSE activities would be absorbed.

A third way in which PSE services appear to be very important is where community demands for services are changing and the inflexibility of regularly budgeted functions prevents a speedy response to those changes. Governments are sometimes unable to adapt to changes in the needs and preferences of the community because of the skill mix of employees or the work rules. For these governments the value of added flexibility may be quite high. These governments can use PSE workers to expand services in areas where public demand is newly revealed or anticipated, even when it cannot reduce other services that are less in demand.

Several jurisdictions assigned PSE workers to do things that local officials and department managers regarded as critical but that they had been unable to get done because of institutional rigidities. Taking slots away from accounting and adding new slots for bike path construction usually takes time. It is equally difficult to transfer positions from the fire department to the police department. We are unable to determine just how much the value of PSE is enhanced in these situations, but in many instances associates said that the PSE program came "just in time" to let jurisdictions meet more varied service needs.

In summary, local flexibility to use PSE for community services may result in services that the community values highly. These services are likely to be less valuable than those that are regularly funded, but the difference may be small. The view of PSE as "work relief" tends to undervalue PSE, much as some analyses of the employment program of the depression of the 1930s overlooked the value of the public works it provided. Furthermore, if governments can use PSE participants for needed services, they are more likely to cooperate in reaching other PSE objectives.

Wages of PSE Participants

The kinds of jobs created by PSE and the types of services provided to the community are reflected in the wages paid to participants. CETA requires that PSE participants be paid the same wages as regular employees working in similar positions, so wage limitations also become limitations on services. These wage limitations are critical, however, to the success of the program as countercyclical or structural policy. The higher the wages paid, the more likely that skilled workers who could find unsubsidized employment will be hired as PSE participants. Such a program would fall short of the PSE design in two respects. First, it would not direct jobs to those most in need of employment and training. Second, it might foster greater wage inflation by bidding for the more skilled workers for whom the labor market is already relatively tight.

At the time of the field study observation the maximum allowable wage payment for any participant from PSE funds was $10,000 a year, or $4.83 an hour for full-time work at forty hours a week. Because slightly higher hourly wages could be paid if the workweek were shortened or vacation time allowed, the effective hourly maximum was nearly $5.00 an hour. If a jurisdiction wanted to pay wages above this rate, it had to use its own money to make up the supplement.

The mean wage by occupation for the study sample jurisdictions in December 1977 is shown in table 4-7. A majority of those wage rates were less than the PSE maximum without supplementation. Moreover, as shown in table 4-4, about 70 percent of all participants in the sample were in the lowest-wage occupational categories. It is evident that the vast majority of sample participants were paid less than the PSE maximum, although considerably more than the minimum wage.

There were notable wage differences among classes of jurisdictions. In general, wages were highest in the large distressed cities, particularly in occupations that are most likely to be unionized, and lowest in the rural areas. Generally these wage differences seem to reflect the local differences in regular wage scales and wage levels among jurisdictional types. Table 4-8 compares wages in sustainment and project positions. Wages are higher in the sustainment positions, which are more apt to be in the

Table 4-7. *Average Hourly Wages of Public Service Employment Participants in Sample Jurisdictions by Occupation and Class of Jurisdiction, December 1977*[a]

	Average hourly wage, public service employment participants (dollars)			
Occupation	Distressed large cities	Other large cities	Small cities and suburban areas	Rural areas
Managerial	4.41	5.10	5.12	4.31
Administrative	5.11	4.80	4.90	4.24
Professional	5.35	4.95	4.86	4.45
Paraprofessional	3.84	3.96	4.20	3.75
Technical	5.60	4.56	4.69	4.22
Technician	5.04	4.53	4.03	4.17
Clerical	4.29	3.66	3.69	3.09
Craft	4.78	4.39	4.47	4.59
Operative	5.05	4.35	4.02	3.87
Laborer	4.27	4.06	3.80	3.41
Service	4.33	4.15	3.98	3.18

Source: Data reported by Brookings field associates.

a. See table 4-5. The figures in this table are averages, by sample jurisdiction, for those governments where wage data were available.

primary services and to be more like regular employment. These positions are more often subject to wage comparisons with similar jobs, civil service pay regulations, and review by organized labor.

Although the bulk of the wages paid to PSE participants in the study sample were within the legislated limits, some wages came close to the limit and left little flexibility to lower the wage limit without changing the types of PSE jobs provided. The 1978 amendments to CETA, which set a limit on the average wage a jurisdiction could pay its PSE workers, required an average wage that was lower than the average PSE worker wage at that time.[2] The law also requires that the PSE wage be at least equal to the federal minimum wage and as high as the prevailing local rates of pay for persons employed in similar occupations.

This combination of federal restrictions on wages creates a wage squeeze at the local level, restricting the types of jobs that can be created. In many jurisdictions the prevailing entry wages in most occupations in 1977 were above the allowable average under the 1978 amendments and

2. The 1978 amendments set the maximum average annual federally supported wage at $7,200, with local adjustments up or down to be based on regional wage indexes.

Table 4-8. *Average Hourly Wages of Public Service Employment Participants in Sample Jurisdictions by Occupation, Class of Jurisdiction, and Type of Position, December 1977*

	Average hourly wage, public service employment participant (dollars)							
	Distressed large cities		Other large cities		Small cities and suburban areas		Rural areas	
Occupation	Sustainment positions	Project positions	Sustainment positions	Project positions	Sustainment positions	Project positions	Sustainment positions	Project positions
Managerial	*	4.61	5.20	*	5.32	4.71	4.31	*
Administrative	5.48	4.83	4.91	4.66	4.75	4.75	4.24	*
Professional	5.55	4.62	5.30	4.69	4.74	4.94	4.45	4.93
Paraprofessional	4.02	4.00	4.15	3.96	3.80	4.45	3.75	4.12
Technical	5.98	*	4.97	4.02	4.68	4.54	*	*
Technician	5.23	*	4.64	4.36	4.35	3.89	4.16	*
Clerical	4.38	4.04	3.62	3.72	3.66	3.57	3.08	3.55
Craft	4.97	4.65	6.06	4.07	4.47	4.39	4.63	*
Operative	5.21	4.50	4.54	4.33	4.03	3.79	3.84	*
Laborer	4.53	4.35	4.10	3.95	3.88	3.83	3.41	3.62
Service	4.66	3.83	4.24	3.86	4.13	3.65	3.18	2.98

Source: Data reported by Brookings field associates. The wages are unweighted means of the average wages of sample jurisdictions within each jurisdictional class.
* So few areas reported wages for positions in these occupations that the wage data are not reported here.

some exceeded the maximum. This leaves local governments little room to maneuver within the regulations. The existence of wage restrictions severely hampers the ability of local governments to use PSE for highly valued services. If a local government must lower wages, it may have to sacrifice some local objectives. The difficulty is in keeping the wage level high enough to allow for the creation of meaningful local jobs while not allowing it to get so high that PSE becomes a significant inflationary force.

If a jurisdiction were solely interested in keeping wages low, it could do several things. It could place more of its PSE positions with nonprofit organizations, where wages are generally lower. Or it could set up more special projects for the unskilled, create additional special trainee or aide positions to avoid wage comparisons, and bring in more participants in the eighteen-to-twenty-two age group. Some of these changes are possible in some localities, but others are not.[3] Even if these program changes are accomplished, their advisability may be questioned. For example, should PSE expand among the nonprofit agencies at the expense of local governments, particularly if training and transition opportunities for PSE participants employed by nonprofit organizations are substantially less? Such a shift might also lessen the value of the public services provided. Moreover, if all the PSE positions must be in the low-pay occupations, does this reduce the on-the-job training opportunities and the value of public services provided? Finally, with the host of other programs now focused on youth employment problems, is it wise to steer PSE toward serving youths?

In some jurisdictions and government departments, these questions are moot because local governments face constraints that are not directly under their control or the control of the federal government. Some subcontractors may even refuse to create positions that will meet the wage requirements. The unemployed and disadvantaged may have alternative income sources high enough for them to reject jobs at this pay level. More evident is the problem that local unions of public employees and personnel regulations may simply make it impossible to create government jobs at the stipulated rates of pay. Meeting the wage restrictions will surely result in notable program alterations, including changes in the quality and types of public services.

According to an associate in a large city: "The wage limits and new

3. The preliminary results from the 1979 field study round show that where the lower wage limits from the 1978 amendments were in force, the program tends to be concentrated in nonprofit organizations or in entry-level positions.

eligibility rules have severely limited the ability of the local government to use CETA funds to hire the higher skilled employees it needs." Similarly, an associate in a larger, fiscally distressed city noted:

The average wage restrictions make it difficult for the city to hire craftsmen, firemen, police, journeymen, etc. Hiring within the city has predominately been for custodians, laborers, waste collectors, junior clerks, and dog wardens. All of these are low skill low wage, entry level positions. Without the eligibility or wage requirements it is likely that the city would fill other types of positions with PSE funds. The CBOs [community-based organizations] find the wage regulations to be too low. Some PSEs can make more money on welfare than by working in PSE jobs.

And from another large city the associate reported: "The new PSE wages are below union wages in the city governments. Consequently, virtually all new PSE hiring has been in the non-profits. We doubt that permanent positions in the private sector exist for many of these trainees."

Too little attention has been paid to these effects and to the local situations to which PSE programs must adjust. While it is clear that wages above some level may prevent PSE from attaining its objectives, wages that are too low may also threaten the effective use of the program.

Institutional Effects

Local PSE programs must be shaped and fitted to work within the local environment. Excessive conflict with local institutions threatens the entire program. The task is to create a workable program that serves both federal and local objectives while operating within the established bounds for regular public employment. This is more difficult than some observers appear to recognize. These persons often ask why a certain project cannot be undertaken when it is clearly eligible under the legislation, or why some persons are not hired, or why the wage rate cannot be lowered when there are persons who seem willing to work at lower wages. Such questions assume that the rules of the work place are suspended for PSE, but that is not the case.

Some of the local characteristics to be considered in understanding the potential for PSE in any community include the relationship among the various governments and interest groups within the community, the local wage-setting process in public employment, the nature and strength of public employee unions, and the local civil service or personnel rules. Each of these factors can limit program flexibility and influence PSE in ways that directly affect the extent to which its service objectives can be met.

The institutional setting is difficult to describe and more difficult to classify in a way that allows us to measure and test hypotheses. In fact, most data on the operation of PSE programs do not describe different institutional settings in even a rudimentary way. The analyses provided by the associates for the field evaluation study provide advantages over other research approaches by dealing with these critical institutional questions. While the picture is far from complete, these narratives indicate the effects of local institutions. In particular, they are useful in showing how public employee unions and local civil service and personnel systems influence PSE.

Public Employee Unions and PSE

The effects of public employee unions on PSE can be both direct and indirect. A common direct effect occurs where, as a result of the strength of the local public employee union in combination with PSE regulations requiring payment of comparable wages, PSE employees must be paid union rates. In most cases the participant must also pay union dues, and in some cases program participants are required to join the union. The actual wage received by a PSE employee will depend on the job classification, and wages for all classifications are generally higher where the employees are union members. Unionism also tends to be concentrated in those occupations with higher pay, such as in protective services.

Where unions are strong a PSE worker in a particular functional area and occupation must be paid a certain wage. As long as local governments have flexibility to determine the wage, they can choose which occupations and functions they will assign PSE workers to; when the wage limit is reached, that element of choice disappears. Because wages and fringe benefits tend to be higher in unionized occupations, fewer PSE jobs may be created in those occupations than local governments would otherwise want. Some jurisdictions try to avoid assigning PSE workers to unionized departments, both because of difficulties already encountered and those anticipated.

Here is an excerpt from an associate's report from a small city:

Two years ago, a problem with the union arose because of the question of seniority for a PSE participant in the police department. The question apparently arose with respect to how to count the PSE period of employment.

I inferred from the personnel office that in the future this problem would be avoided simply by not using PSE in the police department.

A similar report came from an associate in a large city: "One interviewee believed that the city avoids unionized job classifications in order to avoid any conflict with union hiring arrangements."

As mentioned above, public employee unionization is highest in such functional areas as protective services, utilities, sanitation, and public works, that is, in the primary services. Where local jurisdictions have found it desirable to minimize or avoid direct contact with unions by placing PSE workers only in nonunionized agencies, public service needs may be sacrificed. Usually, avoidance of unions would reduce PSE employment in primary services.

This problem is partly avoided by local governments where wages can be supplemented or where low-wage, entry-level positions exist. The tables presented earlier in this chapter show that a number of PSE jobs are in the primary service sector, even in the distressed large cities. But further decreases in wage limits would threaten this situation.

Still greater problems may arise if unions or employee associations actively resist the use of PSE. The large number of PSE participants in many governments can scarcely be ignored by their co-workers. It is not surprising that cases arise where program participants are viewed as a threat or even may affect both the design of the program and the productivity of regular employees. One description of such a situation was reported by the associate in a large city:

A lot of conflict developed in the department between permanent employees and CETA people when certain CETA positions were classified as refuse truck driver positions. This is a position that regular refuse laborers work hard to get. Suddenly, a CETA person with only a regular driver's license and no experience in garbage work appears and gets such a job—a job that regular employees view as a promotion.

Similarly, an associate from a small city had this to report:

Until recently, employee associations, especially the ones in the city departments, have not acted as a constraint on kinds of positions created or persons hired. However, with the introduction of VI-P (title VI projects), the eligibility regulations and expansion of participation in the program, opposition by these associations has increased. The program lowers the morale of regular employees who resent some of the treatment given to participants. As a result, this association feels that it must change its previously passive stance and oppose PSE participants completely.

In other areas local officials and unions have cooperated in an attempt to find some way to reconcile the local effort to provide needed services with the federal wage restrictions. One way to do this is to create special job categories that bypass the contract provisions specifying wages for each regular occupation. Often these special categories are "trainee" or "aide" positions, which usually appear in our occupational classification as paraprofessionals and technicians. In a few cases, before PSE, contract provisions and job classification titles allowed for lower wages to be paid for temporary or provisional employees. In some high-wage areas, all PSE employees were given these job titles even though many of them were engaged in the same tasks as regular employees, but this cannot be successfully accomplished without some agreement with the union.

Some unions and employee associations have cooperated by allowing the creation or expansion of such job categories, even openly agreeing that PSE employees will be paid below the usual scale. These agreements foster the creation of the low-paid, temporary employment envisioned by the legislative architects of PSE, while allowing local governments to provide services in the functional areas where they see the greatest need.

In one large city with strong unions the associate reported:

A deal was cut in spring 1979 between city personnel, the unions and City Council, which resulted in the Council passing supplemental legislation which specified the following: (1) PSE will be used only for entry-level jobs; (2) no Civil Service status will be given for PSE workers; and (3) seniority does not accrue until people are absorbed onto the city payroll.

The associate in another large city reported:

An example of an important union concession was an agreement reached by the city with several unions which permitted opening of a pre-apprenticeship training program for wastewater treatment personnel at the CETA maximum wage. The civil service system was able to adjust the regulations to be consistent with CETA (regarding layoffs of CETA employees, causing them to be eligible for open city jobs).

It is understandable, however, that employee groups have not given their wholehearted support to all efforts to create special wage and job classification provisions for PSE workers. Any arrangement allowing low-wage workers to perform essentially the same tasks as regular employees is likely to be viewed as a threat. If unions or employee associations suspect that regular employees are being displaced by this "cheap" labor, they are likely to take strong actions to avoid it. One associate noted that "unions affect the local manpower office in two ways. They push to get laid-off union members reemployed in PSE slots. They also keep the manpower office 'on its toes' with respect to displacement."

Believing that PSE is likely to be around for some time, some groups are making fairly elaborate arrangements for its accommodation. For example, in one large city a public employee union has reached an extensive agreement with the CETA prime sponsor that applies to all PSE employees in the jurisdiction. The four main provisions of the agreement are (1) PSE positions are not included in the seniority and promotion list; (2) all positions are entry level and pay less than union scale; (3) PSE employees are not union members, but they must pay a fee to the union for grievance representation; and (4) the availability of PSE participants shall in no way place constraints on the expansion of the regular work force.

The agreement is an attempt to permit the development of a job creation program for the unemployed and disadvantaged while protecting regular employees. With the 1978 amendments to CETA in force, the development of such agreements may be critical to the success of PSE, especially to the highly valued aspect of service provision. At the same time, such agreements strike directly at the local opportunity to use PSE funds for displacement, since strict adherence to item 4 would prevent the use of funds for that purpose. This suggests that there is local as well as federal pressure to use PSE as a true job expansion program.

Personnel and Civil Service Systems

Although the local government may have more control over personnel and civil service system regulations than over union contract provisions, their operating rules may also constrain PSE activities. In some sample jurisdictions even the entry wages for a few occupations exceeded the maximum allowable PSE wage. According to a report from one large city "the civil service pay scale is too high to allow PSE employees to work for the city in some categories under the prevailing wage requirement."

Civil service regulations may also impede the implementation of PSE by requiring tests and minimum qualifications of new employees. Many in the PSE target population have difficulty meeting the employment standards. Local officials are sometimes reluctant to propose that these entrance requirements be relaxed for PSE participants since this may be taken as evidence that the requirements are not really job related. Some officials have defended their entry requirements in the face of discrimination charges, and they may see real danger in arguing for temporary changes to accommodate PSE.

Civil service rules, entrance requirements, and pay rates by occupational classification generally have been developed over many decades. Where they have resulted in a workable system, workers as well as civil service managers resist sudden changes in these rules. While efforts to accommodate PSE are developing, the more dominant picture is one of trying to fit a program into a local institutional setting that may not be flexible enough to handle it. The associate in one large city described a situation that illustrates the difficulty:

The civil service system is too inflexible. Departments and agencies can't develop new tasks, new titles, or new activities within the system. All positions, PSE and otherwise, must fit into an existing job classification. Consequently, if you give totally different tasks to a PSE employee than you have given to a regular employee with the same job title, you demoralize your regular staff. The effort to do something new, different, or imaginative is thus greatly hindered by civil service.

The effects of unions and civil service systems are most evident in the large cities where the rules have a longer history and tend to be more rigid. Public employee unions are also more influential in these cities, especially in the eastern metropolitan areas. There probably are no jurisdictions where local institutional constraints are absent, however. One great strength of decentralized programming, such as that for CETA programs, is that it allows local officials to alter programs to meet the demands of their local institutions. Federal overseers may not always feel that the results help attain federal goals, but these local institutions cannot be assumed away. In the next phase of the field study more attention will be given to potential institutions and historical relationships in an attempt to further ascertain how local institutions influence PSE.

Summary and Conclusions

When the provision of public services is seen as an important local program objective, it follows that it is important in shaping the types of jobs created and the participants hired. The field study data show that PSE positions are heavily concentrated in the primary services. That is particularly true for the positions retained by local governments and those in the sustainment portion of PSE. Even so, participants in all categories usually hold low-pay, low-skill jobs.

Some of the services provided through PSE are apparently quite important to the community as well as to local officials. If that is so, the benefits from PSE may be considerably understated when PSE is seen as only countercyclical or structural policy. But the analysis of public services is doubly important because the incentive to maximize those services promotes local cooperation in the program. Attention to public services may also promote some of the structural objectives of the program. When the output is highly valued, the jobs are more like "real" jobs, where training is promoted and transition is more likely.

Two sets of forces limit the opportunity for local areas to use PSE for local services, however. First, governments must comply with federal restrictions, particularly the wage limitations. Second, governments must implement the program within the existing local institutional framework, including the rules of public employee organizations and personnel systems. As wage restrictions become more stringent, some way must be found to accommodate the local restrictions or the program may be drastically altered. Even though the local program is and will continue to be "bounded" by federal and local constraints, governments must maintain some choice within those bounds. An important lesson from observing the PSE system is that the objectives are interdependent. Since implementation of PSE is a local responsibility, local incentives and objectives, including public service provision, must be considered in program design and analysis.

CHAPTER FIVE

Subsidizing Employment in the Nonprofit Sector

JANET GALCHICK *and* MICHAEL WISEMAN

THE PUBLIC job creation component of the Carter administration's economic stimulus package in 1977 was the first federal effort to use extragovernmental agencies—nonprofit organizations—for job creation on a large scale.[1] In administering the stimulus package, the Labor Department instructed its regional offices that prime sponsors should try to allocate one-third of their title VI funds to nonprofit organizations.[2] Data collected from the second round of the public service employment field study show that as of December 1977 the sample governments, on the average, were exceeding this goal. Although the study did not produce data on the proportion of funds going to nonprofit agencies, it did find that such agencies had 10 percent of the PSE sustainment positions and 43 percent of the project positions.

While large-scale participation of nonprofit organizations in PSE was new in 1977, their involvement in employment and training programs was not. The war-on-poverty ideology of the 1960s had already fostered the use of nonprofit organizations in poverty policy, including employment

THIS CHAPTER is based on data from field research for Brookings and on other research on the PSE program in San Francisco conducted by Michael Wiseman. The authors are, respectively, Research Associate at the Woodrow Wilson School of Public and International Affairs at Princeton University and Associate Professor of Economics at the University of California at Berkeley.

1. The designation "nonprofit organization" is conferred by the U.S. Internal Revenue Service to a wide variety of organizations qualified as exempt from federal income taxation under the provisions of section 501 of the Internal Revenue Code of 1954.

2. U.S. Department of Labor, Employment and Training Administration, *Field Memorandum No. 316-77* (Department of Labor, June 17, 1977).

and training efforts.[3] A primary objective of the war on poverty was to use organizations outside traditional governmental structures in developing poverty-related policy. Designers of antipoverty strategy expected neighborhood-based community action agencies to involve the poor in making political decisions and in allocating federal poverty funds. This approach, its designers hoped, would make federal programs more effective and more responsive to community needs. Similarly war-on-poverty advocates claimed that community-based organizations (CBOs) were best suited to locating appropriate target groups and conducting effective training programs. By the late 1960s organizations providing these services had grown in size, experience, and lobbying capability. Indeed, in many jurisdictions these agencies were virtually the only contractors available for providing certain types of training-related services. Additional importance was derived by some from affiliation with national organizations of considerable political influence. These circumstances gave them an inside track even though the Comprehensive Employment and Training Act of 1973 shifted most policymaking authority to the local level. Congress supported this special access by encouraging the use of CBOs as providers of "comprehensive manpower services" and by referring to several prominent agencies by name in defining the term "community-based organization."[4]

Although they were active in training-related programs, CBOs and other nonprofit agencies were only marginally involved in job creation policies before Congress passed the Emergency Jobs Program Extension Act in 1976. For the most part, participation of nonprofit agencies in job creation programs had not been of major concern to federal or local officials nor, for that matter, even to the nonprofit organizations themselves. As funding for PSE became larger relative to funding for the training titles, however, the interest of nonprofit organizations increased.

The greater attention to PSE by nonprofit organizations coincided with growing congressional concern about the targeting of PSE on the disadvantaged and the problem of displacement—that is, the use by local government officials of subsidized jobholders in place of persons who would otherwise have been hired using local money. Those who wished to im-

3. For a brief historical summary see Maurice A. Dawkins, "The Role of Community Based Organizations in Manpower Policy Programs," in National Commission for Manpower Policy, *Community Based Organizations in Manpower Programs and Policy*, Special Report 18 (NCMP, 1977), pp. 71–94.
4. Sections 101 and 601(a)(1), P.L. 93-203, December 28, 1973.

prove the targeting and job creation impact of PSE cited several reasons for greater use of nonprofit organizations, especially CBOs. They argued that community-based nonprofit organizations would be better able to get subsidized jobs to people most in need. They contended that by placing subsidized jobs in nonprofit organizations that were already doing training and job placement, the government would make it easier for participants to acquire skills and ultimately permanent jobs. They pointed out that eventually the opportunities for local government employment expansion would be exhausted; as this point was approached, more might be gained by putting the jobs in the nonprofit sector. Moreover, they noted that nonprofit organizations might be more flexible in designing jobs and using PSE workers than local governments, especially those constrained by rigid civil service systems. Advocates of using nonprofit organizations argued that many of these agencies provide useful services to the communities or groups from which PSE participants are to be drawn. Subsidizing employment within these organizations would increase the flow of such services.

Even though some government officials had reservations about giving up PSE jobs to nonprofit organizations, few local government representatives objected to the use of such agencies while Congress was debating the 1976 extension act. The silence of opponents probably testifies more to the political influence of the nationwide CBOs that had participated in training programs in the 1960s and of community action agencies than to the intrinsic strength of the case for their participation. Certainly in 1976 and at the time the stimulus package was funded, the usefulness of additional employment in the nonprofit sector and the ability of these organizations to meet the needs of the Comprehensive Employment and Training Act target groups was very much an open question. The principal argument used by proponents of nonprofit agency participation, including the agencies themselves, was that the national organizations already listed in the original CETA legislation as preferred providers of training services had a record of "demonstrated effectiveness" in employment and training activities. No one could be certain in advance, however, that effectiveness in providing training is the same thing as, or is even related to, effectiveness in providing jobs. Despite its importance, this issue was rendered largely irrelevant by subsequent developments. Few of the training organizations that lobbied so hard to expand PSE's outreach to the nonprofit sector actually obtained PSE-funded employees.

National and Local Organizations

Table 5-1 shows that 25 percent of the 61,828 positions included in all
PSE titles in the field sample were allocated to nonprofit organizations as
of December 1977.[5] Differences by title reflect the growing importance
of nonprofit organizations in PSE job creation, since all of the project
(title VI) hires occurred in 1977.

We use the term "national nonprofit organization" for two types of
agencies. The first includes all agencies affiliated with a national organization that exerts some control over its local affiliates' management and operation.[6] The second is made up of nonprofit organizations that have been
designated "community action agencies" and receive support from the
Community Services Administration, the successor to the Office of Economic Opportunity. Although community action agencies are quasi-
independent, they are represented on the national level by the CSA itself.
The organizations explicitly recognized in CETA legislation as CBOs are
Service, Employment, Redevelopment (SER) Jobs for Progress; Opportunities Industrialization Centers (OIC); Urban Leagues; and community action agencies. They fall in the general "national" category.[7]

Classified in this way national nonprofit organizations played only a
minor role in the economic stimulus program expansion. Although nonprofit agencies as a whole provided a large share of the jobs created in
the 1977 program expansion, the national group accounted for less than
one-tenth of such jobs. The national CBOs were very poorly represented.
Only 5 percent of total sustainment positions and 3 percent of project

5. The study sample could understate the degree of participation by nonprofit
organizations under CETA. The data are drawn from a sample of governments, not
prime sponsors. In areas in which the sampled government was not also the prime
sponsor, the data will not include positions directly allocated to nonprofit organizations by the prime sponsor unit. This effect is likely to be slight, however, because
twenty-two of the forty-one units sampled were prime sponsors. These twenty-two
prime sponsors account for 97 percent of all employment covered by the sample.
When the tabulations are confined to the subset of data from prime sponsors only,
the results do not change.

6. Designation of national organizations was based on citation in Margaret Fisk,
ed., *Encyclopedia of Associations*, 11th ed. (Gale Research, 1977), vol. 1.

7. Units of local government designated community action agencies are not included as nonprofit agencies. In some cases designation of agencies was based on the
authors' judgment, given fragmentary evidence in the associate reports.

Table 5-1. *Nonprofit Organization Positions in Public Service Employment in Sample Jurisdictions, December 1977*

Type of position	Total public service employment positions	Positions in nonprofit organizations			Nonprofit organizations as percent of total	National nonprofit organizations as percent of total
		All	Local	National		
Sustainment	33,785	3,417	2,944	473	10	1
Project	28,043	12,044	9,994	2,050	43	7
All	61,828	15,461	12,938	2,523	25	4

Source: Authors' calculations based on data reported by Brookings field associates.

positions went to nonprofit organizations from this group of experienced deliverers of employment and training services. The major role was played by a diverse collection of bit players ranging in character from the Coalition of Concerned Women in the War on Crime to Gay Community Services, Inc. One jurisdiction reported allocations to 267 different nonprofit organizations in the projects portion of the program alone.

These data indicate that the stimulus package pushed PSE into uncharted territory for employment policy. Although the experienced training organizations claiming "demonstrated effectiveness" have created an image of what nonprofit organizations are like, the track record and character of new organizations, or for that matter the older organizations under PSE, are not well established. In this chapter we investigate some issues in evaluating these developments, using data from one of the sample cities, San Francisco. We then compare results for San Francisco with reports by field associates on nonprofit performance at other sites. Our evidence on the consequence of relying on nonprofit organizations is not conclusive. It does, however, pose serious questions about the usefulness of the nonprofit sector as an instrument for PSE expansion.

The Role of Nonprofit Organizations in CETA Job Creation

Subsidized employment is a means to three ends: reducing joblessness among certain groups of workers, enhancing their skills, and producing public services. The various types of job programs share these objectives but differ in emphasis. A purely "countercyclical" PSE program has as its primary objective hiring workers who are least likely to compete for other jobs. This minimizes any inflationary effect on wages. A "structural" PSE program is oriented more toward enhancing skills and improving the earnings of disadvantaged workers. For both types of policies the value of the services provided may be an important consideration in weighing the costs and benefits of the program. Whatever the mix of objectives, evaluating nonprofit organizations in job creation programs involves comparing their success in attaining these objectives with that of the local governments that are the mainstay of PSE.

In assessing the outcomes of PSE in the nonprofit sector one must examine the quality of targeting jobs on preferred recipients, the net impact of the subsidies on agency employment and services, and the long-run effects on the well-being of jobholders. These outcomes are affected by three components of the CETA process: selection of agencies, contract specification, and agency implementation. The selection process involves the procedures followed by prime sponsors or other units of government in choosing nonprofit organizations for participation under CETA. The contract defines the terms of this participation. Implementation covers what the nonprofit organization does with the money given in the contract. By changing selection and contracting procedures, a prime sponsor could possibly change the outcomes—and the relative performance of nonprofit organizations as job creators. Thus the purpose of evaluation is not primarily to make "up or down" judgments about using nonprofit organizations but to identify ways to improve the program at the selection or contract stages.

Categorizing the Nonprofit Agencies

A designation by the Internal Revenue Service of tax-exempt status is no guarantee that an organization will respond to PSE in ways consistent with federal goals. The range of nonprofit organizations is quite broad: from communal religious societies qualifying under section 501(d) of the Internal Revenue Code to "religious, educational or charitable organizations" qualifying under section 501(c)(3), and from "labor, agricultural, and horticultural organizations" qualifying under section 501 (c)(5) to the "black lung benefit trusts" cited in section 501(c)(21). Over 650,000 such organizations have received tax-exempt status.[8] Not

8. Burton Weisbrod, *The Voluntary Nonprofit Sector* (Heath, 1977), p. 20.

all these organizations participate in programs authorized by CETA, but the list of participating agencies reported by the field associates suggests that those that do are quite varied. Thus the list of participating agencies must be divided into categories that are related to how the agencies behave in using their PSE subsidies. If some types of agencies do better, the government can channel more funds into such organizations.

If the PSE contract were completely specified and fully monitored, the characteristics of the organization creating the subsidized jobs would be irrelevant. That is, in return for the CETA subsidy, nonprofit organizations would agree to create a certain kind of job with a certain amount of training services for a certain type of worker who would provide a well-defined service. Nonprofit organizations failing to deliver could be sued, lose their contracts to other organizations, or both.

In practice, PSE objectives and contracts are incompletely specified, and it is not always possible to observe with much precision what job-creating agencies do with the money once they get it.[9] Two agencies may do slightly different things even when both are observing the rules. For example, the costs of supervising new workers must come from the agency's own resources, so one agency may provide close supervision while another may supervise its PSE workers only as closely as its regular workers. To find out how nonprofit organizations implement the PSE programs, then, one must look at their actual behavior, not at written promises. We therefore sought a theory that would identify characteristics of nonprofit organizations that would help predict their behavior when given a CETA employment subsidy.

We have found three such characteristics: (1) the extent to which the agency's principal output is a "public," or "collective," good; (2) the constituency and target group of the organization's normal activities; and (3) the agency's normal function.

The Collective Nature of the Agency's Mission and Output

PSE is intended to benefit the worker as well as the general public. The transfer of income to those on whom a PSE job is targeted as well as some

---

9. For a discussion of the CETA-PSE contract and its deficiencies see Harry Katz and Michael Wiseman, "An Essay on Subsidized Employment in the Public Sector," in *An Interim Report to the Congress of the National Commission for Manpower Policy, Job Creation Through Public Service Employment,* vol. 3: *Commissioned Papers* (NCMP, 1978), pp. 151–234.

of the public services many PSE jobs promise are "collective-consumptive goods." That is, the activity benefits a wide range of people, and the receipt of benefits by one person does not significantly diminish the benefit enjoyed by another. For example, the fact that one person can enjoy a clean street does not reduce the satisfaction enjoyed by his or her neighbor. The transfer of income and the provision of skills associated with PSE jobs are collective goods to the extent that other people benefit when the disadvantaged are assisted.

Nonprofit organizations differ in the degree to which their basic purpose is to produce goods and services that have collective consumption aspects.[10] Some have no collective aspects at all. An artists' marketing collective, a trade union, or a burial society might provide services only to its members. For other organizations, collective goods are the central part of output—the Salvation Army takes care of derelicts for all of us; various ecological organizations are unable to exclude nonmembers from the clean air they help maintain; and if Zero Population Growth lowers the birthrate, all Americans will be affected.

Adherence to federal goals in the use of CETA employment subsidies would appear to impose a greater burden on agencies with little orientation toward collective goods than on agencies traditionally producing such services. In particular, the former may be more prone than others to displace regular employees with those paid for through CETA to free funds for the benefit of their membership. Likewise, an agency that is oriented toward private goods may be less inclined to hire the most disadvantaged PSE workers, because its concern is to provide the best possible service to its members. In doing so such agencies may use the funds in ways at variance with the basic CETA goal of serving the most disadvantaged people and, to the extent possible, providing useful public services.

The Agency's Constituency and Target Group

We define the constituency of a nonprofit organization as the group external to management having the greatest influence on the agency's goals and day-to-day operations. The agency's target is the group or

---

10. See Burton A. Weisbrod, "The Private Nonprofit Sector: What Is It?" University of Wisconsin at Madison, Institute for Research on Poverty, Discussion Paper 416-77 (1977).

groups deriving greatest benefits from its principal services. A central assumption behind CETA regulations is that those community-based organizations with service targets related to the groups intended by Congress to receive CETA services are likely to be most effective in achieving CETA goals.

Community-based nonprofit organizations are not the only agencies, however, that serve the needs of the disadvantaged. Any agency regularly serving the targets of CETA legislation would appear more likely than others to use the subsidies efficiently and in accord with CETA goals.

It is also conceivable that the emphasis on funding local nonprofit organizations, whether community based or not, is inappropriate. Organizations of any type with national affiliation may more rapidly identify with the national objectives implicit in CETA employment programs. Moreover, the publicity associated with inappropriate use may be more costly to national organizations. For either reason such agencies may be more likely than others to use CETA subsidies in a manner consistent with national goals.

The Agency's Normal Function

As discussed above, the CETA regulations emphasize some national organizations because Congress believed that agencies experienced in providing employment and training services were likely to do a superior job with PSE. Thus if the normal function of an organization is to provide employment and training services, the agency may be more likely than others to use CETA subsidies in a manner consistent with national CETA goals.

CETA and the Nonprofit Sector in San Francisco

This round of the PSE field study sample was not designed to evaluate the role of nonprofit organizations in CETA, and as a result the reports of field associates for now are probably more useful as a source of hypotheses than as a source of conclusive judgments. However, for one city, San Francisco, the data collected were sufficiently detailed to investigate some of the issues raised concerning the use of nonprofit organizations. This section summarizes what these data reveal about the consequences of the use of nonprofit organizations in this major jurisdiction.[11] The next section presents a comparison of the use of nonprofit organizations in San Francisco to what associates reported for other cities.

Background

San Francisco is a CETA prime sponsor, and CETA programs in the city are operated by the Mayor's Office of Employment and Training (MOET). Some San Francisco PSE participants have been "outstationed" in nonprofit organizations since as early as 1971. Before the economic stimulus expansion, these allocations were done on an informal basis. The stimulus package brought the city two problems. First, the city had trouble finding the 2,528 subsidized jobs it was required to provide under title VI sustainment before it could start to use the projects money. Obviously city departments could not absorb the number of slots contemplated by the stimulus expansion. Second, some officials feared the projects money would turn out to be a political liability. This concern was based on the expectation (which was justified) that demand for the funds would exceed supply and that therefore some groups would be disappointed and, rightly or wrongly, would blame the mayor. In addition, it was unclear in 1977 just what "projects" amounted to. If the people picked up in these jobs were soon to be laid off, the political benefits from their employment would be lost. MOET decided to isolate the allocation of PSE slots from the mayor's office and to make the process as objective as possible.

On February 23, 1977, MOET published a *Request for Proposals* inviting nonprofit agencies, along with city departments and other units of government to apply for PSE project slots. The proposals were to describe the activity for which CETA support was requested, the jobs to be funded, and the agency's normal functions and budget. MOET received 896 proposals, of which two-thirds were from nonprofit organizations. Table 5-2 shows the distribution of project applications by type of agency.

11. This section draws on and extends materials first discussed in Michael Wiseman, "Studies in Public Service Employment: Project Report," report of the Welfare and Employment Studies Project, Institute of Business and Economic Research (University of California at Berkeley, 1978). A much more detailed study of the behavior of San Francisco's CETA bureaucracy will appear in a forthcoming dissertation by Fritzi Reisner of the Graduate School of Public Policy at Berkeley. The authors acknowledge Reisner's substantial contribution to the analysis that follows.

Table 5-2. *Project Applications for Support under the Comprehensive Employment and Training Act by Agency Type, San Francisco, March 1977*

Item	City and county government	Public schools	Other government	Nonprofit organizations	Total
	Agency type				
Number of applying agencies	28[a]	4	16[b]	314	362
Number of proposals	161	96	32	607	896

Source: Mayor's Office of Employment and Training, San Francisco.
a. City departments counted as separate agencies.
b. Federal branches counted as separate agencies.

MOET ranked each proposal on a series of sixteen criteria (to be discussed below) and recommended funding 375 to the Board of Supervisors. After some slight changes the board approved the list in late June. MOET immediately began negotiating contracts with the participating agencies. Hiring started in September. By December 31, 1977, the observation date for the field study, employment had reached the levels shown in table 5-3. As the table indicates, the nonprofit sector played an important role in the stimulus expansion.

The Applying Agencies

When a nonprofit organization applies for tax exemption under section 501(c)(3) of the Internal Revenue Code, the Internal Revenue Service asks it to choose terms that "describe or most accurately identify" its "pur-

Table 5-3. *Public Service Employment Positions Filled in San Francisco as of December 31, 1977*

Program	City and county government[a]	Public schools	State government	Federal government	Nonprofit organizations	Total
	Job location					
Title II	284	65	2	1	...	352
Title VI sustainment	1,692	153	70	47	200	2,162
Title VI projects	297	48	6	13	709	1,073
Total	2,273	266	78	61	909	3,587

Source: Unpublished participation data provided by the San Francisco Mayor's Office of Employment and Training.
a. Includes city housing and redevelopment agencies.

Table 5-4. *Type and Percentage of Nonprofit Organizations Applying for Public Service Employment Grants, San Francisco, 1977*

Principal activity of nonprofit organization[a]	Percentage	Principal activity of nonprofit organization[a]	Percentage
Religious activities	1.9	Conservation, environmental, and beautification activities	2.9
Schools, colleges, and related activities	7.0	Housing activities	1.0
Cultural, historical, or other educational activities	15.2	Inner-city or community activities	9.9
Other instruction and training activities[b]	8.6	Civil rights activities	1.6
Health services and related activities	7.6	Litigation and legal aid activities	3.8
Business and professional organizations	2.2	Legislative and political activities	1.3
Mutual organizations[c]	1.3	Other activities directed toward individuals[d]	12.1
Employee or membership benefit organizations	1.3	Activities directed to other organizations	2.5
Sports, athletic, recreational, and social activities	1.6	Other purposes and activities	1.6
Youth activities[e]	14.3	Insufficient information to classify	2.2

Source: System of classifications from U.S. Internal Revenue Service; authors have assigned each organization to an IRS classification.

a. Internal Revenue Service classifications.

b. Includes "job training, counseling, and assistance" from IRS "activities directed to individuals" classification.

c. For example, credit unions, mutual insurance companies, and mutual irrigation or electric companies.

d. Excludes "job training, counseling and assistance" and "day care center."

e. Includes "day care center" from IRS "activities directed to individuals" classification.

poses, activities, operations, or type of organization" from a list supplied by the IRS. As the instructions indicate, these descriptors confuse organization types with activities, but they provide a useful instrument for describing the range of organizations that applied to MOET for PSE allocations. Table 5-4 tabulates the nonprofit organizations that applied for San Francisco's PSE money on the basis of the IRS codes. Apparently

Table 5-5. *Four Project Proposals, San Francisco, 1977*

Applying agency	Project	Number of jobs	Response of Mayor's Office of Employment and Training
Travelers Aid	*Tenderloin Center for Children in Crisis:* a child care center for children of families newly arrived in San Francisco and/or living in the tenderloin district.	3	Accepted
Mental Health Association	*Mental Health and the People:* PSE employees to assist in (1) providing opportunities for community education about mental health, (2) assessing community health services, and (3) influencing public policies for improvement of mental health services.	3	Rejected
Civil Service Association, Local 400	*Public Information and Service Program:* PSE employees to assist in gathering and disseminating information of city and county fiscal operations to benefit employees and taxpayers.	2	Rejected
Chinese Culture Foundation	*Neighborhood Arts Services:* PSE employees to assist in coordination of foundation's neighborhood arts services program.	2	Accepted

Source: Project descriptions submitted to Mayor's Office of Employment and Training, San Francisco.

there is a broad range of nonprofit organizations in the city. Total expenditures for fiscal 1977 for these applying organizations was $102 million; total overall city-county government outlays was $900 million.

Most of the nonprofit organizations' proposals involved only a few positiⁿ s (the average was slightly under four) and they were at least as varied in character as were the sponsoring agencies themselves. The projects were predominantly related to social services: 76 percent of the proposals were for health, education, or other social services. Table 5-5 summarizes four of the proposals.

Besides using the IRS categories, we classified applying nonprofit agencies on the basis of the behavioral factors cited earlier. The principal activity of about 15 percent of the agencies was producing private goods —that is, services for members of participating organizations that did not have a collective-good aspect.[12] Most of the agencies were not community based, here defined as having a well-defined geographic or demographic constituency; indeed only about 11 percent were identified with particular neighborhoods and only about 14 percent were associated with particular demographic groups. About 31 percent of the applying organizations had CETA-type training or employment-related services as a principal function. Only 17 percent of the applying organizations were nationally affiliated.

The Selection and Contract Process

The sixteen criteria that MOET used to evaluate proposals were divided into two groups: those covering minimum requirements and those related to less tangible impressions of effectiveness and quality. MOET scored each proposal on each criterion with a number from 1 (best) to 6 (disqualification). Officials then ranked the proposals on the basis of the sum of the scores of all criteria.

Although MOET officials tried to take into account both CETA regulations and qualitative considerations in selecting projects, in practice the "minimum requirements" criteria counted most heavily, for there was much more variance in the ratings given on them. Partly because of pressure to speed the evaluation process MOET evaluators placed considerably more weight on routine requirements of form and organization than they placed on those qualitative factors—placement commitment, quality of training, and market demand for skills imparted—critical to the success of structural policy.

THE CORRELATES OF SUCCESS. To identify the type of nonprofit organization that was able to obtain funds under MOET's selection procedure, we devised a simple model showing what determined whether a proposal was likely to be successful.[13] We found that the MOET criteria favored project proposals that were small relative to overall agency budgets. In

12. We identified agencies as not providing collective goods if more than 75 percent of their operating revenues were derived from the sale of services and if the beneficiaries of their services could not practically prevent persons who did not pay from using the agency's output.

13. The model and estimation results are described in Janet Galchick and Michael Wiseman, "Background Data, Research on Use of Nonprofit Organizations in Job Creating in San Francisco," Welfare and Employment Studies Project Discussion Paper 79-3 (University of California at Berkeley, Institute of Business and Economic Research, 1979).

general the projects creating jobs with relatively high salaries were preferred over projects with low salaries, possibly because high-salary jobs
tended to have other desirable qualities. Also favored were nonprofit
projects targeted toward the city's Asian residents and projects providing
social, educational, or health services.

MOET's choices reveal definite preferences for certain types of agencies. Nonprofit organizations with a specific geographically defined constituency were less likely to be successful than were those whose constituency was not identified with any specific geographic area. On the other
hand agencies with a demographic constituency—that is, those associated
traditionally with certain racial or ethnic groups—were more likely to be
successful.[14] There was no relation between the collective-good orientation of the agency's normal functions and the likelihood that a project it
proposed would obtain funding.

To be sure, these results are perfectly consistent with the interpretation
that Asian-oriented organizations and organizations with city-wide constituencies turned in better proposals than did others. Regardless of the
interpretation, the important point is that the criteria applied by MOET
did direct money toward certain types of projects in certain types of nonprofit organizations. If these agencies are exceptionally bad or exceptionally good in their PSE performance, the overall effect of nonprofit use in
San Francisco will differ from what occurs in the other cities in which
different criteria were applied.

THE CONTRACT. Once the Board of Supervisors accepted the project
list, MOET officials began signing contracts with the agencies that had
been selected. Like most CETA contracts, the MOET agreement was
weakened by the ambiguity of impossible-to-police requirements such as
"participants are . . . [to perform] meaningful and necessary public service work at all times." This ambiguity plus the preoccupation of the
MOET staff with other matters made enforcement of the contracts some-

14. These results were not unwelcome to MOET. At the time projects were being
selected the agency, along with the rest of city government, was undergoing criticism for excessive emphasis on blacks in its affirmative action programs. The strong
showing of Asian groups in the project allocations helped counteract this criticism.
In addition, the voters had just approved a charter amendment that changed the
method of electing the Board of Supervisors from "at large" to district elections. In
this context allocation of grants to organizations with a specific geographic constituency is tantamount to allocations to the constituents of a particular member of
the Board of Supervisors. If this had occurred to a significant extent, MOET would
have faced more problems with the board than was the case given the criteria actually employed.

Table 5-6. *Public Service Employment Participant Characteristics, San Francisco, December 1977*

Participant characteristics	Sustainment positions		Project positions		Nonprofit organization projects[c]		
	All city	City, 1977 hires	City[a]	Nonprofit organizations[b]	Training[d]	National[e]	Community[f]
Female (percent)	36	38	35	48*	47	57*	49
Years of education (mean)	13.9	13.8	14.1	15.2*	15.1	16.9*	14.6**
Less than 30 years old (percent)	53	61	59	58	65**	61	50**
Nonwhite (percent)	75	75	71	55**	63**	47**	75**
Weeks employed at time of entry (mean)	44.4	35.7	57.4*	52.9	50.8	43.2**	50.1
Receiving public assistance (percent)	16	17	12*	10	8	4**	11
Reported number of dependents (mean)	1.14	0.86	0.75*	0.44**	0.41	0.37	0.53
Addendum:							
Number of observations	1,989	978	260	693	230	78	186

Source: Authors' tabulations of participant data provided by the Mayor's Office of Employment and Training, San Francisco.
a. Tests of significance are for difference from all city sustainment hires.
b. Tests of significance are for difference from city project hires.
c. Tests of significance are for difference from projects not of indicated organization type.
d. Nonprofit organizations providing employment preparation and training services.
e. Nonprofit organizations affiliated with national organizations.
f. Community-based organizations with demographically or geographically defined constituencies.
* Significant difference at 0.10 level of confidence.
** Significant difference at 0.05 level of confidence.

what lax. But it should be pointed out that many of the ambiguous restrictions were lifted verbatim from the *Federal Register*. By December
1977, the reference date for the Brookings field study, the city had 1,073
people employed in projects; two-thirds of these were working for nonprofit organizations.

The Outcomes

No data are available that are suitable for evaluating the ultimate effects of the stimulus money on the incomes of PSE participants in San
Francisco. At the time this chapter was written (fall 1979), many of the
persons hired in 1977 had not left the program. Useful data do exist on
intermediate outcomes: characteristics of persons hired and an independent evaluation of project implementation done by San Francisco's
Board of Supervisors.

PARTICIPANT CHARACTERISTICS. Data on education, age, race, sex,
and other characteristics for PSE participants are not an infallible indi-
cator of the degree of targeting of PSE programs, because some nonmi-
nority, well-educated persons are eligible for and need subsidized employment. However, if local government agencies hire people who are
noticeably different from those hired by nonprofit agencies at the same
time for the same program (and in the same labor market), it is reason-
able to attribute the discrepancy to differences in agency objectives and
possibly to differences in the kinds of jobs created and the skills required
to fill them.

To evaluate the targeting of PSE in the nonprofit sector in San Francisco, we tabulated eight characteristics of participants for various types
of employing agencies. Four of the variables related to demographic information. These include sex (identified by percentage of participants
who are female), age (identified by percentage of participants less than
thirty years old), education, and race (identified by percentage who are
nonwhite, including Hispanic persons). The remaining three variables are
related to economic status and are measured as of the time the participant entered the program. These include weeks unemployed, whether the
participant is from a household that received public assistance through
aid to families with dependent children or general assistance programs,
and number of reported dependents.

Table 5-6 shows the characteristics of San Francisco's PSE participants enrolled as of December 31, 1977, by CETA title and employing

agency.[15] Characteristics of persons hired during 1977 are separately identified for city sustainment positions. For projects, characteristics of employees in nonprofit organizations and city government are separately tabulated. All project employees were hired during 1977.

The following conclusions seem to be supported by the data in the first four columns of table 5-6:

PSE workers hired by nonprofit organizations are more likely than those hired by regular city departments to be white females with college educations. Persons filling project jobs in nonprofit agencies showed a high level of education; in fact, MOET data show that four out of five had educations beyond high school. Nonprofit organizations were significantly less likely to hire members of minority groups than were city government departments.

Other tabulations show that among minority groups the projects provided more jobs for Asians than for blacks, and this differs significantly from hiring ratios within city government. Moreover, the proportion of welfare recipients hired by nonprofit organizations was significantly lower than the proportion of welfare recipients among all 1977 hires in city sustainment positions.

When they enter the program, PSE participants are asked to report the number of dependents they have, not including themselves. These reports provide some information on the effect of PSE wages on the well-being of persons other than the participant. The average PSE participant in San Francisco city government reports about one dependent. The mean for 1977 hires in city government (see table 5-6) is less—0.86 in sustainment positions and 0.75 in project slots. For project jobs in nonprofit organizations the average number of dependents per participant is less than half the overall PSE city government average. Almost eight out of ten (78 percent) of public service employees in nonprofit organizations reported no dependents at all.

These dependency ratios may simply reflect the greater proportion of women in nonprofit organization employment. When the number of dependents by employing agency was analyzed for women only, however, the result was the same.

The differences in participant characteristics between government and nonprofit agencies may have been due to differences in the type of positions offered by each type of employing agency. For this reason the char-

15. PSE workers in the school district or other governments are not included.

acteristics of persons holding secretarial-clerical positions—a relatively homogeneous occupation—were tabulated by agency. Once again the results were the same: 90 percent of persons holding PSE jobs of this type in nonprofit organizations reported more than a high school education, while only 48 percent of city PSE jobholders in this classification did. Thirty-seven percent of secretarial-clerical PSE jobholders in the nonprofit agencies were white; only 21 percent of city jobholders were white. Nonprofit agencies in San Francisco appear to target their hiring less than do regular city government agencies.

It is also possible to investigate the characteristics of participants in projects "on the margin." As employment expansion continues, does targeting deteriorate or improve? The answer appears to be neither. No significant difference could be identified between hires in the best projects by MOET's criteria and those that are closer to the margin of acceptability. The more marginal projects tended to hire more blacks and fewer Asians or whites.

Although these results strongly suggest that nonprofit organizations have a comparatively poor record in targeting, these particular data may be influenced by the unusual nature of San Francisco itself. Although the city shares many characteristics with other cities, the magnitude of its problems may be overstated by indicators meant to be applicable to the full range of American cities. Some features of San Francisco make it a desirable place to live. Young, better-educated persons with limited work experience may be attracted to the city and as a result may be disproportionately represented as PSE workers in nonprofit social service agencies.

The results reported so far are for all participating nonprofit agencies combined. It is useful to disaggregate the participant data along the lines that we earlier suggested might have behavioral significance. We classified organizations into three types for this purpose: (1) agencies with a community-based (demographic or geographic) constituency, (2) agencies whose principal function is to provide training and job-related services, and (3) agencies with a national affiliation. The disaggregation accomplished by this classification is modest, but it is a step in the direction of identifying whether and how certain types of agencies affect the outcomes of CETA policy. Data classified in this way appear in the last three columns of table 5-6.

The disaggregated nonprofit participant data support several conclusions. Agencies with a formal orientation toward training appear to employ younger workers and workers who are from minority groups more frequently than do others. Like other nonprofit organizations, these agencies do not target PSE jobs on welfare recipients or on workers with dependents as well as the city did with its sustainment slots. The lower dependency ratio could be due to the emphasis on youth, however. Not surprisingly, community-based organizations do hire more minority workers than do other nonprofit organizations; on the average, the workers they employ appear more disadvantaged, reporting less education and more dependents and greater frequency of welfare receipt than do participants in other nonprofit organizations. Only the difference in minority proportions and education is statistically significant, however. Finally, the table speaks strongest on the issue of home-based versus national affiliates. On the average, targeting was much worse for nationally affiliated organizations. Note that the categories are not mutually exclusive: some nationally affiliated organizations do employment and training work, and these agencies tended to hire in the same manner as other training-oriented nonprofit agencies.

BOARD OF SUPERVISORS EVALUATION PROJECT. In the fall of 1977 the San Francisco Board of Supervisors asked its budget analyst to study PSE implementation in the nonprofit organizations that had received project allocations from the stimulus funds. The study was undertaken with staff hired with PSE money. The analyst's report was issued on February 6, 1978.[16] The style of the evaluation was zealous and explicitly patterned after those of the General Accounting Office. The report is used here to provide elements of a study of PSE outcomes.

The board's analysts made on-site visits to 202 of the projects funded by MOET and evaluated each on the basis of five criteria: (1) source of referrals for PSE hires, (2) maintenance of separate bank accounts for CETA funds, (3) compliance with record-keeping and reporting requirements, (4) appropriate use of CETA-subsidized personnel, and (5) resources and organizational support provided PSE jobholders. Criteria one through three relate to compliance with routine requirements. Criterion four was intended to get at the displacement issue. An agency was cited for inappropriate use if it was "using CETA participants to carry out routine agency functions or . . . not addressing the project goal and activities specified by the contract."[17] Criterion five related to the quality

---

16. San Francisco Board of Supervisors, "Monitoring Report of the Comprehensive Employment and Training Act (CETA) Title VI Public Service Employment Projects Operated by Private Nonprofit Organizations" (February 1978), p. 14.
17. Ibid.

of the CETA jobs and whether sponsoring agencies provided adequate supervision, facilities, and training for the participants. The analysts simply gave each project a "problem" or "no problem" ranking on each item. Thus it was possible for a project to receive up to five "bad marks." Most received one, since very few agencies hired from employment service referrals—the test for bad marks on criterion one. The analysts' rating can be used to investigate three questions:

—To what extent did MOET's proposal evaluations detect shortcomings that were related to problems identified by the board's monitoring team once projects were in place?

—Was there any identifiable relation between "bad" rankings by the Board of Supervisors and those agency characteristics hypothesized above to affect behavior?

—Was there any identifiable relation between "bad" rankings by the Board of Supervisors and the characteristics of the people hired by the project?

To answer these questions, we analyzed the board's evaluators' judgments about whether the agency's use of PSE workers was appropriate (criterion 4) and whether its resources were sufficient (criterion 5). Although deficiencies in all five categories could be attributed to the newness of the project approach, the speed at which projects were to be implemented, and the early stage at which the projects were evaluated, the two categories we chose seemed the most likely to reveal fundamental agency shortcomings.

Using these two factors, we compared participant characteristics in problem projects to those in others. We also tried to detect relationships between the probability of a "problem" classification and certain agency and project characteristics. We found no significant correlation between the board's evaluation results and MOET's overall project ranking. Some of the individual criteria used by MOET, however, proved good predictors of the outcome of the board's investigation. For example, those projects that involved activities certain to be completed within a year and were scored well on this characteristic by MOET were exceptionally likely (compared with others) to fall into the board's "bad" category. Apparently the more discrete and separable the projects activity was from the agency's day-to-day functions, the more likely it was to be ill-managed in the opinion of the board's analysts.

MOET's advance evaluation of the quality of training and supervision expected for a project was borne out by the board's results. We found a significant relation between the way MOET rated a project on these criteria and the likelihood that the board's team would cite the project for providing insufficient resources and organizational support for participants. In general both the MOET and the Board of Supervisors evaluations gave projects low marks on quality of training and supervision. The average MOET rating of project proposals from nonprofit organizations was 4.1 on a scale of 1 (best) to 5 (worst). The board's monitoring team reported that for half of the projects examined the sponsoring agency had "not committed sufficient resources to provide new CETA participants with adequate organizational support."[18]

As was the case for MOET's ranking, we detected no significant relationship between the characteristics of persons hired for problem projects and the characteristics of persons hired for other projects. We can infer that in San Francisco, at least, attention to management standards need not imperil the flow of CETA income to disadvantaged households.

The sample of agencies evaluated by the Board of Supervisors team was quite small, so it was difficult to relate evaluation results to agency characteristics. We did find, however, that agencies whose normal functions focused on providing "private goods" were more likely than others to be cited by the board's monitoring team for "inappropriate personnel utilization."[19] The same holds true for projects within agencies that have employment and training as a normal function. A significant positive relationship was also detected between the number of positions assigned to the agency and the likelihood of citation for inappropriate job use.[20]

These relationships and the characterization on which they are based are quite crude. Nonetheless, the results support the contention that there are systematic differences among different types of nonprofit organizations in response to PSE subsidies, and that the outcomes may be related to factors, such as size of project, over which the agency has some control. More work is needed on models of nonprofit agencies to help plan the best ways to subsidize their work.

18. Ibid., p. 11.
19. Ibid., p. 14.
20. The conclusions cited in this paragraph are based on results of estimation of a logit equation relating the probability of citation of an individual project by the Board of Supervisors evaluation project for the problems cited in the text to project and sponsoring organization characteristics. A complete description of these estimation results is available in Galchick and Wiseman, "Background Data."

Summary

We can draw the following conclusions from our study of the use of nonprofit organizations for PSE in San Francisco:

—Prime sponsor preferences had a significant effect on the selection of nonprofit organizations that applied to participate in PSE. Different preferences would have substantially changed the character of the employing agencies. If agencies of different types use PSE differently, this means that the outcomes from the use of nonprofit organizations in CETA will depend on prime sponsors.

—Nonprofit organizations in San Francisco targeted less than did local government departments.

—Some evidence was found of differences among nonprofit organizations in their commitment to federal goals for PSE that could be related to the character of their normal function.

—San Francisco's evaluation criteria appear to have discriminated against nonprofit organizations with national affiliations. The results of the participant-characteristic tabulations appear to justify this preference.

—The margin for additional expansion of PSE in the nonprofit sector is considerable. We found no evidence that targeting deteriorates as outreach into the nonprofit sector increases, but this may be a result of the ordering of nonprofit organizations imposed by San Francisco's evaluation criteria. Some evidence was found in the Board of Supervisors' evaluation results that, all other things being equal, larger projects were more likely to lead to inappropriate job use than were small ones. This is important, for MOET, like other prime sponsors, is likely to emphasize large projects because they economize on agency effort.

—Both MOET's own evaluation of the nonprofit project proposals and the study done after implementation by the Board of Supervisors suggest that nonprofit organizations used in San Francisco do not excel in providing the kinds of training needed for a structural PSE policy.

The San Francisco results do not provide information on the effect of possible variations in the CETA contract, and no information was available on the effect of PSE on nonprofit organization service delivery. Because of the procedures MOET used, this countercyclical program took a long time to start—close to eight months. Some of the delay, however, was caused by special circumstances unlikely to be present in the future.

Nonprofit Public Service Employment Elsewhere

Although the data about nonprofit organizations in San Francisco provide important clues to the role of these organizations in other prime sponsor jurisdictions, by itself the evaluation is limited because it may not apply anywhere outside San Francisco. Federal rules and regulations are the same for everyone. Yet these rules and regulations are interpreted by prime sponsor officials who have different attitudes about the program and who are subject to a variety of different local constraints. In this section we analyze nonprofit data for other prime sponsors in the field study sample. Although these data are imperfect at best, we can combine them with the San Francisco data and draw some tentative conclusions about nonprofit effectiveness in the PSE program.

Attitudes and Policy Choice

Federal policy and regulations generally fail to distinguish the different roles that nonprofit organizations can play in employment and training programs. By contrast, the field associates' reports for prime sponsor jurisdictions suggest that local officials apparently have clear notions about what should be expected from nonprofit agencies within their jurisdictions.

We tried to classify the prime sponsor jurisdictions included in the sample by the most prevalent attitude the jurisdiction's officials had toward organization involvement in the project portion of PSE—the part of the program in which the federal government encouraged greater use of nonprofit agencies. Although it is not always easy to identify any single rationale for using or not using nonprofit organizations, three major attitudes seemed to predominate among prime sponsors adopting a positive attitude toward their involvement.

As might be expected, officials who favored using nonprofit organizations felt they had a commitment to serving the long-term unemployed or other disadvantaged target groups. For example, the associate in one large city reported: "The selection of community-based organizations as subcontractors under project PSE insures the continued targeting of funds towards the minority disadvantaged."

Because the project approach also was to be implemented as part of a countercyclical program, officials in a number of jurisdictions (including San Francisco) saw the use of nonprofit organizations as the best way to hire a large number of persons quickly. For these governments the countercyclical strategy became the most important consideration in the use of nonprofit agencies. As one associate put it:

The city and other governments were not hiring nearly enough title VI participants to achieve hiring goals by the end of 1977. The PSE managers decided to sharply increase the number of slots to nonprofit organizations. Fortuitously, the Department of Labor was also calling for substantial nonprofit involvement in PSE. The city far exceeded the national policy target for nonprofits.

A third reported reason for involvement of nonprofit agencies was political: some nonprofit organizations were viewed as having the necessary local political influence to ensure a role for themselves. For example, in one city the associate maintained that the city council was "aware of the political clout of some CBOs."

Although these three attitudes favor a larger role for nonprofit organizations, a fair proportion of prime sponsors would not have used these organizations without the federal requirement. Moreover, no associate reported that local officials viewed nonprofit agencies as a primary means of meeting local public service needs. Apparently governmental jurisdictions—not nonprofit organizations—are considered to be more important when public services are emphasized under PSE. Governments that put more emphasis on public services and also are less likely to use nonprofit agencies in many cases are fiscally distressed jurisdictions that need PSE to provide essential services. But a similar tendency was evident in relatively well-off suburban jurisdictions that were attracted to PSE by the possibility of enhancing the level of public services.

The differences in attitudes reported by field associates are to some extent reflected in the proportion of project positions that the prime sponsor actually allocated to this sector. Table 5-7 shows that prime sponsors whose officials had a "countercyclical strategy"—those who wanted to fill many positions quickly—tended to involve nonprofit agencies most frequently. Almost twice the percentage of project positions on the average were going to nonprofit organizations in these jurisdictions than the Department of Labor required. The association of nonprofit organizations with target groups also ensured a slightly larger than mandated role for such organizations. Prime sponsors that did not want the involvement of nonprofit organizations did not use them as much as did others with more positive attitudes.

Table 5-7. *Allocation of Project Positions to Nonprofit Agencies by Reason, Selected Sample Jurisdictions, 1977*

Reported reason for use of nonprofit agencies	Mean percentage of positions allocated to nonprofit agencies[a]
To serve target groups ($n = 7$)	37
To fill many positions quickly ($n = 5$)	59
Agencies have political influence ($n = 2$)	28
Prefers not to use nonprofit agencies ($n = 5$)	19

Source: Data reported by Brookings field associates, nineteen jurisdictions included.
a. Unweighted; includes some positions allocated but not yet filled as of December 31, 1977.

Political influence alone was not enough to ensure a large role for nonprofit organizations during the economic stimulus expansion of programs. One reason is that they had not been large employers of participants before that time. Some associates reported, however, that the stimulus expansion did establish an important precedent for nonprofit organizations, and these associates predicted more competition for funding in the future.

Project Evaluations

The analysis of San Francisco data suggested that both the project proposal evaluation criteria per se and the act of rating project proposals on the basis of these criteria affected the kinds of nonprofit organizations likely to receive project funding. How similar was this evaluation procedure to that used by other prime sponsors? How useful are these kinds of evaluations in filtering nonprofit agencies?

In the regulations governing the administration of the project portion of PSE, the Department of Labor required all prime sponsors to solicit and evaluate project proposals for possible funding. In doing so prime sponsors were required to ensure that federal law would not be violated; for example, jurisdictions had to maintain their local level of tax effort, and private profit-making organizations could not receive funds. Otherwise prime sponsors had some latitude in designing and using an evaluation system.

Point systems similar to San Francisco's appeared to be a popular method of ranking proposals. But other jurisdictions were more likely to separate "minimum project requirements" from criteria that were more comparative in nature. In these cases the minimum requirements were not extensive and did not become part of the relative rankings that were ultimately used to choose among proposals.

Aside from the differences in the treatment of minimum requirements and weights attached to individual criteria, the evaluation criteria of the different jurisdictions generally dealt with similar issues. Most jurisdictions set criteria having to do with structural aspects of the program—the targeting, training, and transition of participants. Yet these criteria were almost always broadly stated, and they were seldom accompanied by guidelines to help proposal evaluators assign points in a uniform way. For example, several jurisdictions gave more points to projects that had a commitment to hiring the unskilled. But virtually none of these jurisdictions provided guidance as to precisely how many participants in what types of occupations constituted such a commitment. Moreover, some criteria concerned "serving the target groups." Yet few evaluations stipulated exactly which target groups should be given priority.

The general lack of specificity in the rating of project proposals has several results. First, the evaluation procedure loses some ability to distinguish between project proposals that meet federal requirements and explicit local objectives and those that do not. Second, as demonstrated in San Francisco, lack of specificity in evaluating goals may lead evaluators to give exceptional weight to mere procedural matters as they allocate funds. Third, ambiguity in the selection process reduces the likelihood that the contract between the prime sponsor and the nonprofit organization will be tightly specified and properly implemented.

We emphasize that the project approach was a new and large-scale venture for both the prime sponsors that evaluated proposals and for the nonprofit organizations that submitted and implemented them. Nonetheless, many of the problems identified in these kinds of evaluations may be inherent in the process itself and may reappear should federal countercyclical policy once again mandate a massive buildup in the number of PSE jobs.

The Participating Organizations

The field data do not allow us to describe in detail the process by which the project evaluations result in the choice of nonprofit organizations for funding. But we can compare in a general way the choices in other prime sponsors with those of San Francisco.

We have already seen that both in San Francisco and in all prime
sponsors in our sample national nonprofit organizations received fewer
PSE positions than did local organizations. The national training organizations that had their roots in the poverty programs of the 1960s and
whose influence was a key factor in the expanded role for nonprofit agencies under PSE received even fewer positions. There are several possible
reasons for this development. First, the number of local organizations
available to apply for PSE allocations far exceeds the number of available
"nationals."[21] On the average, however, national organizations would
tend to be larger in size and would be more likely to meet at least the minimum requirements for receipt of PSE allocations. Second, it is possible
that many national nonprofit organizations simply did not apply for PSE
funding. But evidence from the field reports suggests that it was not un-
common for prime sponsors to solicit individual organizations for project
proposals. Given this practice, it is unlikely that suitable national organizations would have been ignored. Third, some observers have suggested
that local affiliates of national organizations may not have the flexibility
to deviate much from the policies set at headquarters—and tailoring job
requests to the needs of the prime sponsor may require a considerable degree of flexibility.

A fourth possible reason for the relatively poor showing of national
organizations as PSE employers is that they may have been of greater
value in an alternative role. For seven of the prime sponsor jurisdictions
in our sample, national organizations were used as "umbrella organizations." In most instances these umbrella organizations handled the allocation of positions among other nonprofit agencies. They also played a
key role in PSE implementation in the nonprofit sector by coordinating
participant selection and referral, by keeping enrollment and payroll records, and by providing technical assistance to other nonprofit organizations.

There seem to be two basic reasons for using such umbrella organizations. The first is a matter of competence. In some jurisdictions the umbrella organization helped the prime sponsor administer a much expanded
program, especially by giving technical and administrative assistance to
the new players in PSE—the smaller, local nonprofit agencies. The second is a matter of politics. The use of umbrella organizations to allocate

21. Approximately 14,000 national organizations are listed in Fisk, *Encyclopedia
of Associations.* This amounts to slightly over 2 percent of Weisbrod's estimate of
the number of existing national and local nonprofit organizations.

positions or to administer the program, or to do both, reduced political pressure on the prime sponsor.

These national nonprofit organizations therefore tend to have their greatest impact in program administration rather than in directly providing employment and training. Prime sponsors apparently preferred to use national organizations in this way. Whether this "guidance" function led to the provision of more or fewer jobs to the disadvantaged than would otherwise have been the case is not clear.

The Contracts

An important aspect of the contract between prime sponsors and non-profit organizations is the specification of how much money will be allocated for administrative purposes. The CETA regulations allowed up to 15 percent of the grant to be used for administration and related matters.[22] These allowances are used for two primary purposes: hiring staff to handle enrollment and payroll records, and hiring staff to supervise and train participants.

Evidence from the field reports suggests that the actual proportion allocated has ranged from zero to the full allowable amount. An across-the-board allocation of an administrative allowance to all PSE subcontractors is more the exception than the rule. Several jurisdictions, including San Francisco, provided no administrative allowances to nonprofit organizations. In some governments the reason for keeping administrative costs low was quite straightforward: the less spent on administration, the more would be available to pay participants. In other jurisdictions participants in a number of nonprofit organizations were considered to be outstationed employees of either the prime sponsor or an umbrella agency. Whether outstationing was done for administrative convenience or political considerations, a common result was that the nonprofit employer's grant covered only the wages and fringe benefits the workers were paid.

When prime sponsors do not provide administrative allowances to nonprofit organizations, these organizations can only provide extra supervision or training for PSE workers if they commit non-CETA funds to do it. Under this circumstance the nature of the employing nonprofit organization itself—the agency's normal function and objectives—becomes

22. Allowable federal costs for the PSE stimulus expansion are described in "Allowable Federal Costs," *Federal Register*, vol. 42 (October 18, 1977), pp. 55763–66.

Table 5-8. *Characteristics of Public Service Employment Participants by Class of Jurisdiction, Agency, and Program Type, Selected Prime Sponsors in the Study Sample, December 1977*

Unweighted average percentages

Participant characteristic[a]	Large distressed cities (n = 8)				Other large cities (n = 8)				Small cities and suburban counties (n = 6)			
	Government		Nonprofit		Government		Nonprofit		Government		Nonprofit	
	S	P	S	P	S	P	S	P	S	P	S	P
Male	71	70	66	62	65	65	41	57	54	52	38	42
Nonwhite	60	71	52	70	62	66	48	49	24	23	31	25
Less than 22 years old	20	22	25	15	24	22	11	13	21	18	9	10
Less than 12 years of schooling	28	28	27	22	15	15	4	13	27	25	23	16
Unemployed 15 or more of previous 20 weeks	54	88	62	94	58	77	77	76	39	58	47	65
Unemployed less than 15 of previous weeks	42	5	38	2	18	21	42	24	34	24	20	9
Family receives AFDC	18	35	4	28	6	8	12	9	7	4	13	5
Family income less than 70 percent of "lower living standard"	45	75	55	85	67	75	66	75	36	38	56	68
Economically disadvantaged	63	87	55	90	67	81	76	79	64	62	65	80

Source: Authors' calculations based on data reported by Brookings field associates.
a. Characteristics are defined as of the time of the participants' entry into the program.
S = Sustainment positions.
P = Project positions.
AFDC = Aid to families with dependent children.

an important determinant of whether it provides additional supervision and training.

Outcomes: Targeting, Training, and Transition

Analysis of participant characteristics in San Francisco raised serious doubts about the ability of nonprofit organizations, especially national organizations, to be more effective than governmental units in targeting on the structurally disadvantaged. The question remains, however: Is San Francisco an unusual case, or does this interpretation hold up in other prime sponsors as well?

The field associates collected data on participant characteristics of enrollees as of December 1977 (see table 5-8). Although these data may be biased because the characteristics reported in the larger jurisdictions reflect particular agencies selected for sampling, this information does provide important points of comparison with the San Francisco data.

The most striking finding relates to the age, race, sex, and educational attainment of the participants. In all types of jurisdictions, larger percentages of participants in nonprofit organizations are female, white, relatively old, and well educated than are participants employed in government agencies. This appears to be true for both the sustainment and the project portions of the program. The notable exception to this tendency occurs in suburban prime sponsors. Nonprofit organizations in these jurisdictions employed a greater percentage of minorities than did government agencies.

That demographic characteristics are skewed in favor of older, more highly educated females may reflect the general cultural and social services orientation of the majority of nonprofit agencies. This orientation offsets the kinds of PSE jobs created on a large scale in government and traditionally held by men—those in public works and sanitation, for example. At the same time, the nonprofit agencies may create jobs requiring more skills than those normally needed on governmental street crews, and to fill them they select females who are more well off in terms of age and educational attainment.

Interpreting information on employment history and income is much more difficult because the data do not allow us to control for the length of time that the participants had been enrolled in the program. The rules of PSE participant eligibility had undergone several changes since the start of CETA programs, and this may partly explain why nonprofit agencies were reported to be serving the more disadvantaged in the sustainment portion of the program. Because nonprofit organizations as a whole were not large PSE employers until the stimulus expansion, the income and employment characteristics of their sustainment hires would be expected to be like those of project participants. Half of the new sustainment hires were to meet the stricter eligibility criteria required for all project participants.

Likewise, explaining the pattern of income and employment characteristics for nonprofit and government agencies in the project portion is more complicated because local officials had the flexibility to impose eligibility standards in addition to federal requirements. One finding that does emerge, however, contrasts somewhat with the findings on demographic characteristics. With some exceptions, nonprofit organizations targeted on the basis of income and employment history as much as or more than did governmental units.

On balance these data partly support the San Francisco conclusions about the targeting effectiveness of nonprofit organizations. Such organizations do as well as governments in meeting the eligibility requirements set up in the law—requirements having to do with income and employment status. If targeting on females, minorities, youth, and less-educated individuals is also intended to be part of the commitment of CETA, the record of nonprofit organizations looks less favorable. Aside from exceptional employment of women, such agencies appear to be less likely to serve these groups than are governments.

Although many consider targeting to be the most important factor calling for involving nonprofit organizations in PSE, training is also important in measuring nonprofit success in carrying out structural objectives. Although the field reports do not allow us to compare the training taking place in governments with that in nonprofit organizations, we can evaluate in a general way the importance of training for all types of employing agencies and then make some general observations about training in nonprofit agencies.

The amount of training varies a great deal from jurisdiction to jurisdiction. Field associates for only five of the twenty-two sample prime sponsors reported that their jurisdictions provided good training opportunities for their participants. Seven more prime sponsors provided moderate levels of training, and ten prime sponsors provided few training opportunities.

The level of training provided is apparently not related to the use of nonprofit organizations as employers of PSE workers. When governments were put into high, moderate, and low training categories, the mean level of participants in nonprofit organizations was approximately the same— 25 percent—for each. Two tentative conclusions can be drawn as a result. First, it may be that a large commitment to nonprofit organizations neither promotes nor impedes training opportunities for participants. Second, although prime sponsor allocation criteria usually include training objectives, in practice evaluators apparently do not take such criteria seriously. Otherwise the "high training" sponsors would have had a disproportionate number of jobs in nonprofit organizations.

The field reports also do not allow us to draw strong conclusions about the relative effectiveness of nonprofit organizations in PSE transition efforts—a third important structural objective. It appears, however, that transition opportunities were not being encouraged for governments or nonprofit agencies. This lack of emphasis was due to the federal countercyclical strategy. The field observations occurred at a time when the federal government was encouraging both structural and countercyclical policies simultaneously. The result, intentional or not, was that prime sponsors emphasized the hiring rather than the structural goals of PSE.

Even though local officials were rapidly building up PSE levels, we still found evidence that some of these officials were also reluctant to depend on nonprofit organizations for PSE transition because the nature of the services the agencies provide may not offer a good opportunity for it. Data from San Francisco and from the other prime sponsors show that while the purposes of nonprofit organizations in PSE may be varied, these organizations are largely confined to social service and cultural activities. This concentration limits the types of occupations that can be developed to perform needed tasks. Moreover, by their very nature nonprofit agencies may engage in activities that neither the government nor the private sector will undertake. If participants gain skills and experience that are specific to their jobs in nonprofit agencies, they might not be able to use those skills elsewhere. Innovative uses of PSE participants in nonprofit organizations may therefore ultimately work to the disadvantage of the participants themselves.

Summary

Field associates' reports generally support the conclusions drawn from the San Francisco analysis. In particular, the following points may be emphasized:

—Because federal PSE policy does not clearly distinguish among structural, countercyclical, and public service objectives, the attitudes and preferences of local prime sponsors are important determinants of the extent and character of participation by nonprofit organizations. Although many local officials equate nonprofit organizations with a commitment to serving target groups, actual involvement of nonprofit agencies in 1977 tended to be greatest when local government policy was itself oriented toward countercyclical objectives.

—The project selection procedures used during our observation period were not specific enough to predict what kinds of nonprofit organizations receive funding and what results funded projects will actually produce. Contracts between prime sponsors and nonprofit organizations generally did not specify how an organization must meet federal requirements or local objectives.

—Locally based nonprofit organizations employ far more PSE workers than do national organizations. Nationally affiliated organizations were occasionally used by prime sponsors to coordinate PSE in the nonprofit sector. But the nonprofit organizations seen in Washington are not by and large the agencies that get the job allocations.

—Data from the sample jurisdictions generally support the conclusion based on the San Francisco evidence that nonprofit organizations do not achieve the targeting objectives of PSE as well as do local governments. Whether nonprofit organization training and transition capabilities are better or worse is still debatable because our evidence indicates that these goals were not emphasized in either sector. Fragmentary comparative evidence suggests, however, that the federal government should not change the mix of PSE toward greater placement in nonprofit organizations if it wants to pursue structural objectives.

Implications

The results presented in this chapter have implications for both research and policy. These implications are weak because, as has already been pointed out, they are drawn from data that were collected for other ends.

On the research side, the San Francisco data suggest that there are indeed behavioral differences among different types of nonprofit organizations and that these differences affect performance under PSE. These results need to be verified at other sites, and much more study is needed on the behavior of nonprofit organizations.

On the policy side, if all nonprofit organizations behaved the same way and if the data presented here were the best available for guiding policy, the clearest implication would be that nonprofit agencies have a substantial potential for creating jobs, but the jobs they create are unlikely to be targeted very well. Some degree of targeting is desirable to achieve both structural and countercyclical objectives. Thus these considerations argue either for no involvement of nonprofit organizations at all, highly selective involvement, or involvement only in a short-term employment program that hires workers of any kind who are made jobless by an economic downturn—a countercyclical program.

Recent changes in PSE regulations have strengthened the structural emphasis of the program. Targeting and training provisions are more substantial, the wage limitation has been tightened, and maximum tenure limitations have been imposed. These changes have in many jurisdictions made placement of PSE jobholders more difficult and consequently have increased prime sponsor attention to nonprofit organizations for job creation. The field study data show that unless prime sponsors pay more attention to contract specification and monitoring, the shift to the nonprofit sector will diminish the impact of the new legislation.

Epilogue

TEN MONTHS after the observations reported on in this study were completed, Congress passed the Comprehensive Employment and Training Act Amendments of 1978, which reauthorized all CETA programs and required recipient jurisdictions to give greater emphasis to hiring economically disadvantaged persons. The amendments also imposed new limits on the length of time a participant could stay in the public service employment program and on the use of local funding to supplement federal PSE wages. These changes were intended to shift the program toward serving the most needy individuals and to discourage local governments from using PSE for displacement. Congress also reduced appropriations for PSE. Enrollment, which reached a peak of 755,000 persons in April 1978, dropped to 534,000 in December 1978 and to 397,000 in December 1979.

The PSE program that emerged after the 1978 amendments treated local officials' interests differently than did the program the field associates reported on in 1977. Congress was no longer as interested in helping local governments expand and maintain public services or in creating large numbers of jobs to counter unemployment. Congress placed more emphasis than before on the structural objective—helping long-term unemployed persons find jobs and gain skills. (Most of the decline in enrollment was in title VI, the countercyclical portion of PSE; enrollment in title II, the structural portion, almost doubled between December 1977 and December 1979.)

Local governments found that they were expected to administer a program in which low-skilled persons would make up a larger proportion of the participants than before. At the same time, local jurisdictions were expected to make do with fewer participants in general and to comply with new restrictions on eligibility, wages, and tenure. They were told that their compliance with federal rules would be more rigorously scrutinized.

118

To local officials, the changes in the law and the reduction in program size meant they had to change the kind of program they were operating and the way they administered it. As the effects of the 1978 amendments came to be felt throughout the program, a number of agencies absorbed their PSE slots and cut back or eliminated their participation; they made it clear that they were disappointed with the program. In brief, they stated that there was no longer anything in PSE for them.[1]

Early in 1981 the Reagan administration, as part of its effort to reduce federal spending, proposed to eliminate the PSE program by the end of fiscal 1981. This proposal met with relatively little resistance. We think the reason for this is that the 1978 amendments significantly reduced the value of the program to local operators. State and local governments seemed to be more concerned about proposed reductions in other forms of federal aid. Nonetheless, if the program is ended, several fiscally distressed cities will be forced to make painful adjustments because they have been more likely than better-off cities to assign PSE workers to basic services. This fiscal flow has also become a major lifeline for community-based nonprofit organizations. They too will be especially hard hit if the PSE program is ended or sharply reduced.

1. For a detailed report on the local reaction, see Robert F. Cook and others, *Public Service Employment in Fiscal Year 1980,* Office of Program Evaluation, Employment and Training Administration, U.S. Department of Labor (USDL, April 1981), a report based on a round of field observations conducted in December 1979. A fourth and final round of field observations was conducted in December 1980. A report to the Department of Labor is in preparation.

Sampling Technique for Field
Observations in Large Jurisdictions

IN THE FIRST round of the study we determined that the size of the program and the number of agencies and projects employing public service employment workers in the larger jurisdictions made it difficult to carefully examine the activities of all participants and to interview the heads of the agencies in which they are employed. However, we felt it was important to observe the activities of PSE participants. Therefore we adopted a sampling procedure in the second round for jurisdictions with more than 1,000 PSE participants. We recognized in planning the sampling procedure that there would be no advantage in selecting individual PSE participants for study, because such a large number of agencies and projects would then have to be observed. As a result, we used a sample of *agencies* for the second observation.

For all the jurisdictions with more than 1,000 PSE participants—which included all the large cities and one suburban county—the associates initially told the central staff at Brookings how many persons were enrolled under title II and title VI and how many were enrolled by each type of employing organization, that is, the local government itself, another government agency, a nonprofit agency, and so on. From this information the central staff determined how many positions should be sampled in each of these large jurisdictions. Once the number of positions to be sampled was calculated for each jurisdiction, jobs were distributed proportionally to actual enrollment of workers in the jurisdiction, first by title and then by employing agencies within each title. Specific agencies were then selected for observation to meet the sample requirements.

In some cases the number of participants in a particular agency exceeded the sample requirements, as when 300 participants were performing cleanup operations in the streets department. In these cases we did not allow one agency to account for the entire sample in that category, nor did we exclude it because of its size. Instead, the agency was included in the sample and was actually observed. The associate, however, reported the results as the proportion of the sample that the agency represented in the universe for that title and type of agency in the jurisdiction. In this way it was possible to sample a number of agencies even where the number of participants in each agency was quite large. This procedure implies that the number of positions actually examined is greater than the sample numbers reported here.

In the jurisdictions where the procedure was used the sample covers 5,434 participants, or 10 percent, of all the positions in those jurisdictions. Combined with the number of participants in the jurisdictions where sampling was not needed, the data presented in chapter 2 are based on the examination of 9,368 positions, or roughly 15 percent of all the positions in all of the jurisdictions studied.

To calculate the percentages shown in the tables in chapter 2, we multiplied the proportions for sampled positions by the total number of participants for each title and for each type of employing agency within each jurisdiction in which a sampling procedure was used. This procedure was designed to produce an estimate of displacement in each jurisdiction and for the sample as a whole.